MARINA CALDARONE

Marina Caldarone is a freelance
radio drama director who has been actively
involved in actor training in the UK's leading
drama schools for the last twenty years. She
is drama director for Crying Out Loud, a
production company making training CDs for
actors. She is co-compiler of *Actions – The Actors'
Thesaurus*, also published by Nick Hern Books,
and the *Radio Active* collections of monologues
and duologues for the recorded media.

OTHER TITLES IN THIS SERIES

The Good Audition Guides

CLASSICAL MONOLOGUES FOR WOMEN

edited and introduced by

MARINA CALDARONE

NICK HERN BOOKS
London
www.nickhernbooks.co.uk

A NICK HERN BOOK

The Good Audition Guides:
Classical Monologues for Women
first published in Great Britain in 2006
by Nick Hern Books Limited
14 Larden Road, London W3 7ST

Reprinted 2008, 2009

Introduction copyright © 2006 Marina Caldarone
Copyright in this selection © 2006 Nick Hern Books Ltd

Cover design: www.energydesignstudio.com

Typeset by Country Setting, Kingsdown, Kent, CT14 8ES
Printed in Great Britain by CPI Antony Rowe, Chippenham

A CIP catalogue record for this book
is available from the British Library

ISBN   978 1 85459 870 7

FSC
Mixed Sources
Product group from well-managed
forests and other controlled sources
Cert no. SGS-COC-2953
www.fsc.org
© 1996 Forest Stewardship Council

Thanks to Rose Bruford College Research Fund and John
Collis, who ran the Learning Resources Centre at Rose
Bruford College, which nourishes so many; Anna Linstrum
and Lindsey Bowden; and Caroline Downing.

Contents

6

8

ACKNOWLEDGEMENTS

The editor and publisher wish to thank the following for permission
to use copyright material:

Electra, Sophocles, trans. Kenneth McLeish, Nick Hern Books;
Hecuba, Euripides, trans. Frank McGuinness, Faber and Faber; *Ion*,
Euripides, trans. David Lan, Methuen Publishing Ltd; *Thebans*, Liz
Lochhead, after Sophocles and Euripides, Nick Hern Books; *Rudens*,
Plautus, trans. Christopher Stace (1981), Cambridge University Press;
Peribanez, Lope de Vega, adapt. Tanya Ronder, Nick Hern Books;
The Misanthrope, Molière, trans. Stephen Mulrine, Nick Hern Books;
The Learned Ladies, Molière, trans. A.R. Waller, adapt. Stephen
Pimlott and Colin Chambers, Nick Hern Books; *Phedra*, Racine, trans.
Julie Rose, Nick Hern Books; *Ghosts*, Henrik Ibsen, trans. Stephen
Mulrine, Nick Hern Books; *The Stronger* (in *Strindberg: The Plays
Volume 1*), August Strindberg, trans. Michael Meyer, Secker and
Warburg; *Miss Julie*, August Strindberg, trans. Kenneth McLeish,
Nick Hern Books; *Uncle Vanya*, Anton Chekhov, trans. Stephen
Mulrine, Nick Hern Books; *The Dance of Death Part II*, August
Strindberg, trans. Stephen Mulrine, Nick Hern Books; *Blood Wedding*,
Federico García Lorca, adapt. Tanya Ronder, Nick Hern Books.

Every effort has been made to trace all copyright holders, but if any has
been inadvertently overlooked, the publishers will be pleased to receive
information and make the necessary arrangements at the first opportunity.

Introduction

AN OPPORTUNITY, NOT A TEST ☞

Let's assume you have an audition coming up. It may be for entrance to drama school, or for your first job after training, or it could be twenty years into your career and you have been asked to show your suitability for a specific role. Whatever the circumstances, the stakes are always high, and the somewhat artificial situation is undeniably nerve-racking. You want to find a monologue that does two jobs at once: it suits your particular skills and it demonstrates your particular suitability for the job you are interviewing for.

Before you begin, it is worth remembering that the person or panel auditioning you is just as anxious . . . for you. They will want to put you at your ease, get the very best out of you, and enable you to enjoy the experience – so that they do as well. Adrenaline can be a useful energising factor, but the most valuable qualities when going into an audition are sound preparation and an ability to flex that most crucial of actors' muscles: the imagination. Dare to make brave choices in the selection and delivery of your audition piece, and you will always stand out. View your audition as an opportunity, not a test.

USING THIS BOOK ☞

The fifty speeches in this volume offer a new selection of classical monologues, divided into five distinct time periods from Ancient Greece to the 1930s. It is not an anthology of 'great speeches from dramatic literature' but, rather, a miscellany of eclectic and original monologues. Many will prove challenging; some will seem immediately unsuitable for you; others will lead you down stimulating new avenues you hadn't considered before. Most of the monologues are taken in their entirety from plays; others have been shaped and moulded from a series of separate but closely connected passages to form a coherent speech.

The monologues are arranged in chronological order, within the five time periods: Classical Greek and Roman, Elizabethan and Jacobean, French and Spanish Golden Age, Restoration and Eighteenth Century, and Nineteenth and Early Twentieth Centuries. Before each section is a short introduction to the respective period, plus some pointers that may prove interesting or useful. By and large, however, the same 'rules' for preparing your monologue apply for all time periods – whether you are delivering Ancient Greek rhetoric, Renaissance tragic verse or savage Wildean wit.

Preceding each individual monologue is a checklist of the basic information you need to know before you can begin work: *Who* is speaking; *Where*; *To whom* and *When* the character is speaking; *What has just happened* in the play to provoke the speech; *What the character wants* and some possible objectives to play. After many of the speeches is a glossary explaining less familiar words and phrases.

This checklist isn't a substitute for reading the play from which the monologue is taken. Nor is it offered as a comprehensive guide or direction on how to rehearse and present the speech. It's a starting point, a springboard, from which you need to start making your own choices, in order to achieve ownership of the monologue and your performance of it.

The important thing is to keep your performance real and truthful. Many people put too much emphasis on the notion of 'classical' text being very different and very much harder than 'contemporary' text. Yes, classical text is harder insofar as the language can be less familiar, the syntax trickier, the form less comfortable – but the heart of the work is exactly the same, albeit sometimes bigger. During the act of transformation, you will need to grow emotionally, linguistically, physically in order to speak these lines; the character remains a person inhabiting a real world – not a 'classical' one frozen in the past!

CHOOSING YOUR MONOLOGUE ☞

There are many books written on how to audition, numerous classes to take in perfecting your audition technique, and it can be easy to forget that the first, and possibly the most important, stage in the process is making your initial choice of audition material.

- You must choose a piece that plays to your personal strengths as an actor; something you know you can understand, can work with, and is within your capabilities as a performer. At the same time, you should be looking to challenge yourself and not confine yourself to any mould. Be brave!

- The speech has to 'speak' to you. You must respond to the text instinctively on some level before you can begin to take it apart. Read different speeches out loud. If you only consider a monologue from an intellectual point of view, there is a limit to what will present itself to you, but in the actual speaking of the words you will taste unexpected nuances. The power of great writing is that you can experience it on an entirely physical level as you swill the text around in your mouth.

- If you are auditioning for a specific role, you must choose one that resonates with or reflects at some level the part you are being seen for. Is it a tragic or comic piece you are auditioning for? What 'weight' is required for the role? Make a judgement and find a monologue that mirrors this dynamic. Is the character emotionally centred, forwardly energetic, or laid-back and relaxed?

- If you are auditioning for a role in a period piece, it makes sense to choose a monologue that is set in the same time period, since you will often be assessed on your ability to speak the language of that period in both a natural and an accurate way.

- Choose a speech that you are excited by, will enjoy working on, and which resonates with you as a performer and as a person. Stay instinctive.

PREPARING YOUR MONOLOGUE ☞

So you've chosen your speech and now need to prepare it for your audition. Here are some of the things you certainly should be doing, some things you might be considering, and some you should definitely be avoiding.

- Always read the play that the monologue is taken from. If you don't, you're hunting for buried treasure without thinking to consult the map. Find out what else the playwright has written, and what identifies the period specifically. This will help you form a context for the monologue and your playing of it, but also give you something to discuss with those auditioning you. An intellectually engaged actor is always an appealing one.

- Find the impulse to start the monologue. Each of the speeches in this volume appears with some suggested objectives as a starting point for you. There must always be a reason for the character to open their mouth, to start talking; there must be something they *want*. A common analogy used is this: If you dive off the diving board in the correct way, you will have a perfect flow through the air and will enter the water effortlessly. Similarly, in an audition, if you don't take a moment to clarify who you are and what you want before diving in, you'll belly flop!

- Once you have your objective/s, one useful way to proceed is to 'action' the speech. Instead of concentrating on acting moods and emotions, you find an active, transitive verb to play on each and every line or objective that helps you achieve your aim. (*Actions – The Actors' Thesaurus,* which I compiled with the actress Maggie Lloyd-Williams, offers an explanation of this widely-used system, and a thesaurus of Actioning words.)

- Consider who the speech is spoken to. It is too off-putting to look directly at the audition panel, so where will you place the person/s you are addressing. Will they move during the speech? Will you 'stage' the piece with movement and gestures, or will you remain static? All the choices you make are crucial in demonstrating your ability to inhabit a role totally.

- The language and syntax of the speech will tell you everything you need to know about the character. We are *how* we *speak*, and *what* we *say*. Look carefully at the choices the playwright has made concerning vocabulary, form and punctuation. A comma is not a full stop; a full stop is not an exclamation mark: they mean completely different things. What does it mean if a character talks rapidly, in short sentences, haltingly, and frequently punctuated, as opposed to one who talks at greater length in a much more florid sentence with rarely a punctuation mark intruding on the text? Be precise in your reading of these instructions, and follow them. Inhabit the character by allowing the text itself to lead your delivery, your breathing, your tempo. It is too often the case, when I am on an auditioning panel, that when I refer to the text of the speech that the actor in front of me is performing, I see that all the punctuation has been ignored in favour of another, generally easier, way of playing it.

- If you are being considered for a role where the character speaks mostly in verse, it would be wise to choose a monologue in verse, and show some working knowledge of how to speak it. The character expresses him or herself in verse for a reason. It's a heightened form, used when prose is not enough to convey their elevated thoughts and feelings. In a musical, a character breaks into song when spoken words are not enough. In drama, verse occurs where prose is not enough. It says a lot about a character when they move from prose to verse within a scene – or even a single speech – and vice versa. Understand and enjoy the change.

- Many of the monologues in this volume are written in iambic pentameter, the most common verse form of the Renaissance theatre. Feel your pulse now or imagine an amplified heartbeat, the short beat followed by the long – the heart pumping blood around your body does so with the rhythm of an *iamb*. So an iambic pentameter consists of a short beat, and then a long one, five times a line. De-dum de-dum de-dum de-dum de-dum. Be careful though: much verse in iambic pentameter doesn't conform rigidly to this pattern. In such cases, don't compress the beats into too regular a five-beat rhythm. The variations are important and intentional, and irregularity can reflect the character's state of mind.

- Classical text must not sound 'classical', it's in the present tense and active, and should sound as if you are speaking it today. We've all heard actors using a false, declamatory voice when performing Shakespeare. Avoid this at all costs in auditions. It is phoney and indicates an actor's ignorance of what the character is actually saying. Speak with immediacy, vitality and truth, and it will be (electrifyingly) powerful.

- The *effort* you put into preparing your monologue will be commensurate with the *effortlessness* it will appear to have in the playing. The French for 'to rehearse' is *'répéter'*. You won't go far wrong repeating and repeating your monologue, trying something different each time, keeping what you like, what 'fits', and letting go what doesn't. It is quite simple: the more fully prepared you are, the more confident you will be; the more confident you are, the more risks you will take, and the more you will 'let go' and be able to respond to any re-direction offered to you.

- However, don't overwork and overanalyse the monologue and your performance of it to the point where it becomes unnatural or forced. Ensure that all your choices are sound, based on taking appropriate time to investigate and rehearse.

PREPARING FOR YOUR AUDITION ☞

- As well as reading the play from which the monologue is taken, you should also read and research the play and the role you are auditioning for.

- Be mindful of the time limit of any speeches you are to present; two minutes is the average length for most auditions. Many of the speeches in this volume will last longer than this, but are offered here in full so you can make your own choices about which passages to play and which to cut.

• Look online for up-to-date information about those who are auditioning you. It may be that you have seen their work, which might help build a picture of what their tastes are, and give you something to talk about.

• You are your own marketing manager. Have good, professional photographs taken and then ensure that the photograph you submit captures you – not just that it *looks* like you, but that it captures your spirit and personality *energetically*. Your agent and your friends can advise you on which photos do you justice. You will lose audition opportunities otherwise, and waste the auditions you *are* invited to.

IN THE AUDITION ☞

• Wear something that the audition panel might remember you by – just wearing black is dangerous. After a day of seeing dozens of people, all of a specific physical type, it can be difficult to remember individual faces, appearances – and performances. At the same time, always dress appropriately for the part you are being considered for.

• Be in good time. A perennially late actor is a perennially unemployed one.

• Be open and positive, polite and friendly; say 'Yes' in your demeanour. That said, neediness is unattractive. Be enthusiastic but not desperate. It can be a fine line.

• Introduce yourself politely and in a professional manner. Take a moment or two to find your centre, and collect your thoughts before you begin your monologue. Always keep breathing!

• Be prepared to be asked to stop, start again, and try different approaches. It doesn't mean your interpretation was wrong; it's just that the person or panel auditioning wants to see how well you take direction and how flexible and creative you are.

AFTER THE AUDITION ☞

If you get through the audition, get recalled, or get offered the job or the drama-school place, then congratulations; the hard work paid off!

But always remember that even if you're not successful this time, you may not have lost the opportunity to work with members of the panel again. Very often a role will be offered to an actor who most closely matches the physical appearance that the director envisaged. You can do nothing about this, so don't carry the disappointment or resentment over to the next audition or opportunity.

If you are rigorous in your approach, creative in your choices, exact in your playing and comprehension of the monologue, and a pleasure to spend those few minutes with, then you will be remembered for future jobs or recommended to others. And that's something you can do everything about. So relax, start work, and enjoy the experience. Good luck!

A NOTE ON THE TEXT ☞

Many of the following monologues are assembled from successive speeches. Where dialogue has been omitted, the omission is indicated by [. . .].

Classical Greek and Roman

The Greek tragedies drew on existing myths and wrapped them up in contemporary Greek history. They are cautionary tales of how to live in what the Greeks considered a brave new world of civilisation. By contrast, the comedies are akin to situation comedies, and generally play anarchically within very established social hierarchies.

The Greeks lived in a world very different from ours today. It was savaged by war, a brutal time when life was cheap. Women were lesser citizens and slaves were people you could practically buy off a shelf. The gods controlled everything and everyone, even sometimes coming to earth to mate with mortals and breed demi-gods. Human sacrifice to the gods was considered normal, and a dialogue could be conducted with them via the Oracles, the soothsayers and the visionaries.

The dramas are huge in their sheer sweep of narrative, and graphic in their depiction of violence. Audiences would pass out at a messenger's description of a horrific death in messy, Tarantino-style detail. The plays were performed in the open air, often in enormous theatres, and with the actors (all male) wearing full face masks.

In the plays of ancient Athens and Rome, psychology is less important than story, and what characters and themes represent. When acting, it's difficult and unhelpful to play a theme or a representation, but it is important to bear your character's *function* in mind. Finding this function is subjective; there are no right or wrong choices. In her speech, Electra could represent, for example, the avenging spirit of Justice.

Don't be put off by the fact that the characters are high born, often royalty. Playwrights chose characters whom their audience would relate to as the best of themselves. The stories would be *about* them, but they would also be sufficiently removed from the characters to learn the 'lesson' of the drama and experience the cathartic power of the work. The audience is actually represented by the chorus, the commonsense voice of reasonable men (and women).

The use of masks would have fostered a highly stylised and formalised method of presentation. But today, classical plays are performed in all manner of different styles: epic, domestic, naturalistic or broadly comic. The monologues that follow here would serve a whole variety of differing presentational styles.

Electra

Sophocles (c. 415 BC), *trans. Kenneth McLeish*

WHO ☞ *Electra, living as a beggar though the young daughter of the Queen of Argos. Sister to Orestes. 20s.*

WHERE ☞ *An open courtyard outside the palace of Mycenae in Argos.*

TO WHOM ☞ *To the ashes of her supposed dead brother. The chorus, the bearer of the ashes and his friend are present.*

WHEN ☞ *Ten years after the end of the Trojan war, around 1300 BC.*

WHAT HAS JUST HAPPENED ☞ *Electra is in mourning for the murder of her father, Agamemnon, butchered by her mother Clytemnestra and her consort on his return from the Trojan War. Electra's one hope was that her brother, Orestes, who had been sent away for his own safety, would avenge the death. But news has arrived that he has been killed abroad in a chariot race, and she has just been presented with an urn containing her beloved brother's ashes. All her hopes have died along with him. She does not know that the reports of his death were false to ensure his safety and that he is actually the bearer of the ashes. So moving is the speech that it prompts him to reveal his true identity.*

WHAT SHE WANTS/OBJECTIVES TO PLAY ☞

- *To be at peace, that this unbearable suffering will cease. To beg his spirit to take her with him to the underworld.*
- *To ask her brother's spirit for forgiveness – she feels responsible for his death amongst strangers. An ignoble and unendurable situation.*
- *To pay homage to the great man that was her brother. To offer due funeral rights in his honour that would not have been paid at his death.*
- *To blame the gods for their irresponsibility in not preventing his being sent away after their father's death.*

Electra

❝ I loved you more than anyone alive, dearest Orestes,
and here is all that remains of you, all that remains
of all my hopes when I let you leave.
A dear radiant little boy when I sent you away,
what are you now? A handful of dust.
I wish to God I had died earlier
before I rescued you and sent you into exile
in a foreign land, to protect you from being killed.
At least if you had died on the same day as your father,
you and he could have shared a family tomb.
But, as it is, abroad, a distant exile,
you died a wretched death, parted from your sister.
My loving hands had no chance to wash you
nor pick out your charred bones, as is only right,
from the all-consuming flames.
Someone did this you never even knew,
and all that's left for me is a little ash in a little urn.
All that looking after you when you were small –
and what a sweet labour it was – completely wasted!
You were never your mother's child. You were mine.
At home you had no other nurse but me, your sister.
In the space of one short day all this has disappeared,
because you are dead. A storm passed over us
and blew it all away. Father's gone.
I am dead if you are, and now you're dead and gone.
Our enemies are laughing at us, and Mother –
no mother at all – is mad with joy,
after you had so often sent secret messages
that you would come and punish her for me.
But bitter fate, both yours and mine, has stolen all away,
sending me instead of your beloved self,
cold ash and insubstantial shadow.
Oimoi! Moi!
O demas oikrton, pheu pheu!
What a terrible path you travelled. Your death is my death.
Oimoi moi! Yes, my death, dearest brother.
Welcome me then to this house of yours

I, who am nothing, to become nothing.
I shall live with you below for the rest of time.
When you were here above I shared all with you equally,
now I want to die and share your tomb;
for I see the dead are without sorrow. **99**

Oimoi! Moi!   pronounced OY! MOY! MOY!
o demas oikrton, pheu pheu!   pronounced OH DEH-mas OYK-tron, FEW
   FEW!

Hecuba

Euripides (c. 424 BC), *trans. Frank McGuinness*

WHO ☞   *Polyxena, daughter of Hecuba, early 20s.*

WHERE ☞   *By the Trojan women's prisoner-of-war camp, near the shoreline.*

TO WHOM ☞   *Odysseus, the Greek Commander in the presence of her mother and the chorus of prisoners.*

WHEN ☞   *Set around 1300 BC.*

WHAT HAS JUST HAPPENED ☞   *Hecuba and her daughter Polyxena, together with large numbers of Trojan women, are prisoners of war after the Greek's victory at the first great war between the east and the west. As revenge for the killing of Achilles, the Greek people demand the sacrifice of the Trojan princess Polyxena. Odysseus has arrived to take her to her sacrifice. Hecuba has just pleaded with him to spare her, and then Polyxena intervenes.*

WHAT SHE WANTS/OBJECTIVES TO PLAY ☞

- *To take control of her destiny by asking to be allowed to go to her death, rather than suffer further humiliations at the hands of the Greeks.*
- *To let her mother know that she is at peace with her decision; that she does not want to live in this world any more.*
- *To reclaim her power whilst she has breath in her body.*
- *To diminish the authority of Odysseus, by undermining his expectations that she might ask for clemency.*
- *To defend her lineage and demonstrate how proud she is to have been born a Trojan woman.*

Polyxena

" Odysseus, you turn your face away.
Your hands harden in the folds of your robe.
You're afraid I might touch you.
Don't trouble your good self.
You are not Zeus – I am no supplicant.
I will troop after you because I must,
And because I long for death.
That is what I choose.
I am no weak – no coward of a woman.
Why should I live – why?

My father was king of great Troy.
That was where I started my life.
I was reared well to be a king's bride.
Princes would fight for that pleasure –
Whose hearth and home would I come to?

The women of Troy once worshipped me,
One like the gods, though I would die.
Young girls praised my now unfortunate name.
I stand here in slavery. Slave – slave –
The very sound makes me long to die.
It's not a name I entertain easily.
What is in store for the sister of Hector?
A cruel master, the smell of his money,
Buying my body to lick his floors clean,
Grind corn in his house, weave at his loom.
I'll serve my hard labour among strangers.
Some other slave ransacked from God knows where,
He'll stain my bed, once the dream of kings.
I will not serve – that will not happen.
I look into the sun, my eyes are my own.
I let go of light, give myself to death.
Odysseus, march me on my way, kill me.
Neither hope nor happiness wait for me.
Mother, say nor do nothing – let me go.

Respect my wish to die before dishonour.
I do not deserve this disgrace.
The path is hard, but I can walk it.
Better dead than alive when life –
Life is toil and torture and hardship. **99**

GLOSSARY

Zeus the king of the gods
Hector Polyxena's brother, the Trojan warrior killed by Achilles

Ion

Euripides (c. 413 BC), *trans. David Lan*

WHO ☞   *Creusa, childless Queen of Athens. Late 30s.*

WHERE ☞   *At the oracle of Apollo at Delphi.*

TO WHOM ☞   *A chorus of local people and an old servant.*

WHEN ☞   *A distant and mythical past.*

WHAT HAS JUST HAPPENED ☞   *Creusa arrives at Apollo's temple with her husband, Xuthus, to ask the oracle if she will ever give birth. Years before, she had a child by the God Apollo, whom she abandoned to die. She believes her infertility is a punishment for this. Full of anger for Apollo, she wants to know if her son is still alive. Xuthus enters the shrine and is told the first person he sees as he leaves the shrine will be his son. As he leaves he happens to see Ion, the young caretaker, and claims him as his son. He encourages Ion to return with him to Athens. Eventually, Ion accepts that what the oracle has said must be true and Xuthus arranges a feast to celebrate. Creusa has just found out that Xuthus has been given this child and she has not; she is furious. Her trusted servant suggests she kills Ion while the chorus of locals have offered to kill Xuthus for his dishonour – siring a child outside of his marriage – and for plotting to get the barren Creusa out of their home. The moment is underpinned emotionally by her recollection of the incident that she believed triggered all this misfortune, the rape by Apollo years ago.*

WHAT SHE WANTS/OBJECTIVES TO PLAY ☞

- *To ask how badly can gods behave and still be treated as gods? If gods are immoral where is the moral centre of humanity?*
- *To mourn her loss of innocence, and her life, ruined by men.*
- *To appeal to the wisdom of age in the old servant, and common people in the chorus, to work out her next move.*
- *To release her anguish and voice her despair.*
- *To directly accuse Apollo of taking her innocence by force.*

Creusa

❝ Shall I speak? Some word
will be said. Silence
can't keep. Darkness
will drag into daylight.
If I do as you say
my name's foul
forever. So?
What value's virtue?
Husband . . . betrayed.
Home . . . bespoiled.
No hope of children.
I believed
if I concealed
I was seduced
A baby born
I would be whole . . .
All hope gone.
Good.

By the star-thronged
throne of Zeus,
his sparkling lake,
the truth I'll shriek!
I'll thunder!
Then my heart
won't heave,
my eyes will dry,
I'll breathe.
How gods and men
scheme I'll reveal
how all men, all
are wicked, cruel
torturers of women!

The lyre sings
with seven strings.
You who pluck them
I accuse.

Apollo.
Flowers I gathered,
let them fall
into the folds
of my silk robe.
Gold they shone,
my lap the sun.
Sun glowing through
your honey hair.
My milk white wrists
you grabbed, you
dragged me. I cried:
'Mother!'
Dark the cave.
A rock my bed.
You seared me!
Then so good it was
I thought I was
the god. I was.
Your son, to hide
from my father's eye
I carried to the cave.
Who found him?
Rats gnaw.
Birds peck.
While you who pluck
the seven strings
were singing
your child
died.

From earth's dark heart
on blood hot throne
you spout prophecies.
Hear mine!
The rocks you set your heel on hate you
And the air through which you fly.
The beach where you were born abhors you,
hills revile you, trees, the sea . . . 　**"**

Thebans

Liz Lochhead (2003)
after Sophocles and Euripides (5th century BC)

WHO ☞   *Ismene, sister to Antigone.*

WHERE ☞   *In Thebes.*

TO WHOM ☞   *The chorus.*

WHEN ☞   *In a distant and mythical past.*

WHAT HAS JUST HAPPENED ☞ *It is 10 years since Oedipus blinded himself and went into exile for discovering he had inadvertently killed Laius, his own blood father, and married his own mother, Jokasta. The two had parented twin sons Polyneikes and Eteocles and two daughters, Antigone and Ismene. The twins had agreed to jointly take charge of Thebes, on an alternating annual basis, except it hasn't worked out. The warring twins have slain each other, the city is strewn with corpses, and Jokasta has cut her own throat at the sight of her dead sons. Kreon, Jokasta's brother, has given instruction to bury Eteocles' body with all due rights, and to leave the body of the perpetrator, in his view, Polyneikes, to rot where it lay on the ground. Antigone cannot leave her beloved brother on the road, and she begs her sister to help her bury him. Ismene won't. So Antigone buries him herself, is discovered in the act by Kreon's guards and taken to a cave to be abandoned until death. Meanwhile the prophet Tiresias warns Kreon that further horror will be perpetuated unless he buries Polyneikes and forgives Antigone. He rushes to do so, with his son Haemon, who was to have married Antigone that day, and here Ismene describes the horror that met them at the cave. It is written in an expressly poetic style. If you consider the lay-out a reflection of how the character is thinking, you might use the separations of thought, that is the natural rhythms of her speech, to specifically create character. But it must not sound like poetry – it is real, this is just how she expresses herself.*

WHAT SHE WANTS/OBJECTIVES TO PLAY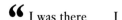

- *To relate it as exactly, as precisely, as she experienced it.*
- *To comfort the people of Thebes in some way. It has all come to an end, the horrors are over. She is the survivor telling this story.*
- *To let the people know that wealth and power count as nothing in the face of such atrocity as has befallen her family.*

Ismene

❝ I was there   I

saw it all
I was with my uncle Kreon
when we got to the body of Polyneikes
what the dogs had left of it

watched
as he washed the torn and stinking carcass of my brother
I tried to help   he snarled   slapped me off
so I stopped   just stood there

watched   couldn't weep
he said a prayer   I moved my lips
as he honoured Polyneikes my brother with
a sweet   a decent   covering mound of earth

then we went running to Antigone
to the cave where   still living   they interred her
by the time we got there
the wall of stones was all but torn away by soldiers
we were sure we could hear   something
someone was shouting deep inside   then silence

slowly
in silence
we walked into the stillness
into the darkness   our torches

Antigone!
Antigone hanging from a rope
my sister   twisted dangling from a
rope fashioned from strips of her own wedding-dress twisted
her slip soaked her trousseau torn
Antigone dangling

Haemon was there he
Haemon howling he
pressed his face to her belly
sobbing
he clutched at her   hugging her
limp lower limbs to him
hanged   Antigone

Antigone
his love   he
pulled out a blade we saw it glinting
he cut the noose   she fell   white   lifeless
broken   he roared
he sprang at his father
spat in his face
his bright dagger at his father's throat

Kreon saw
he stood   would have stood it
would have taken it
accepted it as justice
not lifted a finger
but
Haemon laughed   he turned it
held the blade of the knife towards himself
plunged it
hard into his own body   once

his bursting heart bespattered Antigone
the blood came bubbling
gouts of it   from his loving mouth
as he kissed his Antigone
one last time
and death has heard their vows and married them for ever **"**

Rudens

Plautus (c. 200 BC), *trans. Christopher Stace*

WHO ☞   *Palaestra, daughter of a nobleman, 20s.*

WHERE ☞   *On a deserted beach.*

TO WHOM ☞   *The audience, and also the 'gods'.*

WHEN ☞   *Contemporary with authorship.*

WHAT HAS JUST HAPPENED ☞ *A pimp, Labrax, has absconded with two of his women, Palaestra being one of them, while promising to meet a young Athenian, who has paid a deposit for Palaestra (she was kidnapped by pirates many years ago and sold to the pimp). However, the gods use a storm to shipwreck them and they are separated. Palaestra arrives 'dripping wet and close to exhaustion. Her clothes are in shreds.'*

WHAT SHE WANTS/OBJECTIVES TO PLAY ☞

- *To get the audience 'on side'.*
- *To impress her solid character and blameless life upon the listener.*
- *To convey to the audience her experience of feeling totally lost and alienated by her surroundings – no matter which way she turns, she can find no comfort.*
- *To challenge the Gods for their unfair treatment of her.*

Palaestra

❝ When you hear tales of other people's misery,
You think them bad enough, but they're nothing
Compared with what you suffer in reality!
What have I done so awful that the gods
Have cast me out, in such a frightful state,
A stranger on an unknown shore? Is this

What I was born for, born to misery? Poor me!
Is this a fair reward for having tried
To live a decent life? If I had sinned
Against my parents or the gods, then I would think
All this was fair enough – but no, the truth is quite
The opposite. I have been careful never to offend;
So this is unfair treatment, cruel, unreasonable,
You gods are meting out! If this is how
You treat the innocent, what need the guilty fear?
For if I knew I or my parents had done wrong
To you, I should not think myself so wronged.
But now I am afflicted by my *master's* crimes –
He is the cause of all my misery.
His ship is on the bottom of the sea, and all
He owned. I am the only thing he had
That's left; even the girl who shared the boat with me
Is lost, and I am all alone. If only she were safe
My plight would be less wretched – she could comfort me.
Now what have I left to hope for? I've no help,
No idea where to go . . . in such a lonely spot!
Just roaring sea and rocks – no one will find me here!
These clothes are all I have, no food or hope
Of shelter. What is there left to live for now?
This place is quite unknown to me. If only someone came
And showed me how to find the way! Which way
To go – this way, or that? Oh dear! There's not a field
In sight, no sign of farming hereabouts.
Oh, I shall faint, I'm cold, I'm frightened and I'm *lost*!
My poor, poor parents, if you only knew
How wretched your poor daughter was! Freeborn I was,
Free as the day, and all for *this*! I might as well
Have been a slave for all the use my freedom was,
For all the joy my parents had of me! **99**

Elizabethan and Jacobean

There is no such thing as 'Shakespearian acting', or 'speaking', nor a single 'correct' approach to the work or the words. The work of Shakespeare and his contemporaries is open for constant re-interpretation and re-investigation, and has been produced in as many ways as there have been productions. Any different version will work if the performances are real, and the world created is real.

A recent production of *Romeo and Juliet* by the Icelandic theatre company Vesturport situated the play in a circus ring. The actors playing Romeo and Juliet were trapeze artists conducting every moment of their intricate courtship, with all its linguistic layering and complexities, whilst flying through the air above the heads of the audience. It was a world away from more traditional productions but still beautiful, profoundly moving and true.

The second half of Elizabeth I's reign and the early years of James I's marked an exciting and innovative time for British theatre. One of the key influences was the building of a new kind of playhouse, an open-air amphitheatre. One of the best known of several in Elizabethan London was the Globe, a full-scale working replica of which can be visited today on the South Bank close to its original site. This theatre had an enormous creative and literary influence on the plays written for it. The size of the space necessitated 'big' writing, and the themes were for all people – from the illiterate groundlings who would stand in the yard to watch the play to those better educated and richer who would sit on the various levels. The work was received at various levels too; encouraging writing in which every word is crucial and carefully chosen, and nothing is arbitrary.

In order to release the meaning of these mighty lines, the modern actor must be able to paraphrase each sentence accurately, and play the intentions within. If you break the thoughts up, in an effort to savour each word, you may lose the flow of the sentence's thought and rhythm. Know what you're saying and so will your audience.

In the original productions there were no sets or lighting effects. Everything was to be created in the audience's imagination. So more than in any other genre or era of writing, you have to be able to *visualise* what you are saying, in order that the audience might see it too.

Arden of Faversham

Anon. (1592)

WHO ☞   *Alice, early 20s, married to Arden of the town of Faversham in Kent.*

WHERE ☞   *In Alice's living quarters.*

TO WHOM ☞   *Her lover, Mosby.*

WHEN ☞   *Contemporary with authorship.*

WHAT HAS JUST HAPPENED ☞   *Alice is married to Arden of Faversham. He suspects her of having an ongoing affair with Mosby, but has no proof. Alice meanwhile has been plotting with Mosby to kill Arden. He is a wealthy man and she would stand to inherit his riches.*

Throughout the play Alice is noted for her changeability and her inconstant love – both for her husband and for Mosby. This speech is a typical example of these characteristics. She begins remorseful, and determined to end her relationship and return to being a dutiful wife. But when Mosby responds angrily (in the second line break), ranting that she is a fake, and that she has been a worthless waste of his time, she immediately changes, so that the second half of the speech sees her determined to win back Mosby's love.

WHAT SHE WANTS/OBJECTIVES TO PLAY ☞

- *To end the relationship and put a stop to all plans of murdering her husband.*

- *To express the shame she feels, both personally and publicly, at the affair; and to lay the blame firmly on Mosby, who bewitched and enchanted her.*

- *To renounce all she has said in the first part of the speech, once she realises that his rage suggests he is not prepared to beg her to change her mind, but is likely to abandon his feelings for her.*

- *To reel him back with seductive eloquence and flattery, while attempting to make him grateful of her attention by reminding him, albeit with sugar-coated words, of his humble roots.*

- *To call on all that has been great between them in the past to sustain them now.*

Alice Arden

❝ I pray thee, Mosby, let our springtime wither;
Our harvest else will yield but loathsome weeds.
Forget, I pray thee, what hath passed betwixt us,
For now I blush and tremble at the thoughts.

[MOSBY. What, are you changed?]

Ay, to my former happy life again;
From title of an odious strumpet's name
To honest Arden's wife – not Arden's honest wife.
Ha, Mosby, 'tis thou hast rifled me of that,
And made me sland'rous to all my kin.
Even in my forehead is thy name engraven,
A mean artificer, that low-born name.
I was bewitched; woe worth the hapless hour
And all the causes that enchanted me!

[MOSBY . . . Go, get thee gone, a copesmate for thy hinds!
I am too good to be thy favourite.]

Ay, now I see, and too soon find it true,
Which often hath been told me by my friends,
That Mosby loves me not but for my wealth,
Which too incredulous I ne'er believed.
Nay, hear me speak, Mosby, a word or two;
I'll bite my tongue if it speak bitterly.
Look on me Mosby, or I'll kill myself:
Nothing shall hide me from thy stormy look.
If thou cry war, there is no peace for me;
I will do penance for offending thee,
And burn this prayer book, where I here use
The holy word that had converted me.

See, Mosby, I will tear away the leaves,
And all the leaves, and in this golden cover
Shall thy sweet phrases and thy letters dwell;
And thereon will I chiefly meditate,
And hold no other sect but such devotion.
Wilt thou not look? Is all thy love o'erwhelmed?
Wilt thou not hear? What malice stops thine ears?
Why speaks thou not? What silence ties thy tongue?
Thou hast been sighted as the eagle is,
And heard as quickly as the fearful hare,
And spoke as smoothly as an orator,
When I have bid thee hear, or see, or speak,
And art thou sensible in none of these?
Weigh all thy good turns with this little fault,
And I deserve not Mosby's muddy looks.
A fount once trouble is not thickened still:
Be clear again, I'll ne'er more trouble thee.

[MOSBY. Oh no, I am a base artificer,
My wings are feathered for a lowly flight.
Mosby? Fie, no! not for a thousand pound.
Make love to you? Why, 'tis unpardonable;
We beggars must not breathe where gentles are.]

Sweet Mosby is as gentle as a king,
And I too blind to judge him otherwise.
Flowers do sometimes spring in fallow lands,
Weeds in gardens, roses grow on thorns;
So whatso'er my Mosby's father was,
Himself is valued gentle by his worth. **"**

GLOSSARY

hapless unfortunate
artificer workman, artisan
copesmate companion
sensible capable of sensation
gentles ladies and gentlemen
gentle well-born

Henry VI, Part Three

Willam Shakespeare (1592)

WHO ☞   *Queen Margaret, late 30s or older.*

WHERE ☞   *On a hill towards the end of a battle.*

TO WHOM ☞   *Duke of York, held by her men.*

WHEN ☞   *30 December 1460.*

WHAT HAS JUST HAPPENED ☞   *The Duke of York, with the Earl of Warwick, have stormed the now empty palace in London and taken the throne. King Henry VI enters and York demands the crown. The king tells York that he and his heirs may have the crown after he, Henry, dies a natural death. York agrees. Queen Margaret, angry with her husband for his decision, divorces herself from him, and with her son, Prince Edward, leaves to join the revolting armies of the nobles. At Sandal Castle, York is convinced that his oath not to harm Henry is voided since a magistrate wasn't present when sworn. York plans to attack Henry. However, Queen Margaret arrives with 20,000 men and York still intends to fight, though he and his uncles only have 5,000 men. The battle of Wakefield ensues. This is where the speech comes in. Margaret's men have captured York and she is about to kill him.*

WHAT SHE WANTS/OBJECTIVES TO PLAY ☞

- *To rouse her troops with a triumphant eloquence. To be a man for a moment in the thick of battle.*
- *To humiliate York, and his followers: he has torn her world apart, he will pay for it.*
- *To reinstate her family's right to the throne.*
- *To crush him with the story of his son's death, to destroy him before he is actually killed.*
- *To patronise him, to enjoy toying with him like a cat with a mouse before snuffing out his life, to indulge the sense of omnipotence this fills her with.*

Margaret of Anjou

66 Brave warriors, Clifford and Northumberland,
Come, make him stand upon this molehill here
That raught at mountains with outstretchèd arms,
Yet parted but the shadow with his hand.
(*To York.*) What, was it you that would be England's king?
Was't you that revell'd in our Parliament
And made a preachment of your high descent?
Where are your mess of sons to back you now?
The wanton Edward and the lusty George?
And where's that valiant crook-back prodigy,
Dicky your boy, that with his grumbling voice
Was wont to cheer his dad in mutinies?
Or, with the rest, where is your darling Rutland?
Look, York: I stain'd this napkin with the blood
That valiant Clifford with his rapier's point
Made issue from the bosom of the boy;
And if thine eyes can water for his death,
I give thee this to dry thy cheeks withal.
Alas, poor York! but that I hate thee deadly,
I should lament thy miserable state.
I prithee, grieve, to make me merry, York.
What, hath thy fiery heart so parch'd thine entrails
That not a tear can fall for Rutland's death?
Why art thou patient, man? Thou shouldst be mad;
And I, to make thee mad, do mock thee thus.
Stamp, rave, and fret, that I may sing and dance.
Thou wouldst be fee'd, I see, to make me sport;
York cannot speak unless he wear a crown.
A crown for York! – and, lords, bow low to him.
(*To her men.*) Hold you his hands whilst I do set it on.

She puts a paper crown on York's head.

Ay, marry, sir, now looks he like a king!
Ay, this is he that took King Henry's chair,
And this is he was his adopted heir.
But how is it that great Plantagenet

Is crown'd so soon and broke his solemn oath?
As I bethink me, you should not be king
Till our King Henry had shook hands with death.
And will you pale your head in Henry's glory,
And rob his temples of the diadem,
Now in his life, against your holy oath?
O, 'tis a fault too too unpardonable!
Off with the crown and with the crown his head;
And, whilst we breathe, take time to do him dead. **"**

GLOSSARY

raught reached
preachment sermon
mess gang
crook-back prodigal monstrous hunchback
fee'd paid
pale enclose
diadem crown

Edward III

William Shakespeare (1593)

WHO ☞ *The Countess of Salisbury, playing age 20s or older.*

WHERE ☞ *Castle of Roxborough, where she lives with her husband who is currently fighting for the country in France.*

TO WHOM ☞ *King Edward III. They are alone.*

WHEN ☞ *1340s – during the Hundred Years' War between France and England.*

WHAT HAS JUST HAPPENED ☞ *Upon receiving news that King David of Scotland has seized the Castle of Roxborough, King Edward III has declared war on the Scottish and the threat of retrieving the Castle with his army has frightened the Scots away. The grateful Countess has greeted the newly arrived King, and Edward is very much taken with her. Having been persuaded to stay the night at the castle, he has been trying to conceive a letter that will explain his very real needs for her, carnal though they may be, and his profound and genuine feelings. She interrupts him in this task, and he uses the more direct approach, telling her directly that he wishes to 'have' her. This is her reply.*

WHAT SHE WANTS/OBJECTIVES TO PLAY ☞

- *To let him know in no uncertain terms this is not even a remote possibility.*

- *To make him aware of the bigger political picture, rather than the smaller personal one, namely that his progeny should be conceived honourably and that marriage is a sacred institution.*

- *To remain respectful, not to overstep the line in her refusal. Her eloquence and choice of language is reverential, and is careful not to offend.*

- *To make him aware of his greater duties as a King.*

- *To make him think that she believes she is only being tested for her loyalty to her husband.*

Countess of Salisbury

❝ But that your lips were sacred, my lord,
You would profane the holy name of love.
That love you offer me you cannot give,
For Caesar owes that tribute to his queen;
That love you beg of me I cannot give,
For Sarah owes that duty to her lord.
He that doth clip or counterfeit your stamp
Shall die, my lord; and will your sacred self
Commit high treason against the king of heaven,
To stamp his image in forbidden metal,
Forgetting your allegiance and your oath?
In violating marriage' sacred law,
You break a greater honour than yourself.
To be a king is of a younger house
Than to be married: your progenitor,
Sole reigning Adam on the universe,
By God was honoured for a married man,
But not by him anointed for a king.
It is a penalty to break your statutes,
Though not enacted with your highness' hand;
How much more to infringe the holy act
Made by the mouth of God, seal'd with His hand?
I know my sovereign in my husband's love,
Who now doth loyal service in his wars,
Doth but to try the wife of Salisbury,
Whether she will hear a wanton's tale or no.
Lest being therein guilty by my stay,
From that, not from my liege, I turn away. **❞**

GLOSSARY

profane desecrate
Caesar owes that tribute to his queen the sacrament of marriage applies
    even to monarchs
Sarah owes that duty to her lord 'Even as Sarah obeyed Abraham,
    calling him lord' (1 Peter, 3, 6)
clip devalue
is of a younger house is a more recent title
wanton libertine

The Two Gentlemen of Verona

William Shakespeare (1593)

WHO ☞   *Julia, beloved of Proteus, a gentleman of Verona, 20s.*

WHERE ☞   *In Julia's private chamber. Verona.*

TO WHOM ☞   *Lucetta, her waiting-woman.*

WHEN ☞   *Contemporary with authorship.*

WHAT HAS JUST HAPPENED ☞ *Julia's beloved Proteus has just been sent to Court in Milan by his father. They have had a tearful farewell, but now he has gone, and though she trusts him implicitly, she cannot bear the prospect of being away from him for so long. She decides to get Lucetta, her waiting-woman, to help disguise her as a man in order that she might follow and keep an eye on him.*

WHAT SHE WANTS/OBJECTIVES TO PLAY ☞

- *To win Lucetta over with flattery and genuine regard – but she does need her onside.*
- *To teach the extent to which real love will go.*
- *To warn Lucetta that she will go anyway, it is inevitable – it will be easier with her support than without.*
- *To win her compassion, sympathy and understanding.*

Julia

❝ Counsel, Lucetta. Gentle girl, assist me,
And e'en in kind love I do conjure thee,
Who art the table wherein all my thoughts
Are visibly character'd and engrav'd,
To lesson me, and tell me some good mean
How with my honour I may undertake
A journey to my loving Proteus.

[LUCETTA. Alas, the way is wearisome and long.]

A true devoted pilgrim is not weary
To measure kingdoms with his feeble steps.
Much less shall she that hath love's wings to fly,
And when the flight is made to one so dear,
Of such divine perfection as Sir Proteus.

[LUCETTA. Better forbear till Proteus make return.]

O, know'st thou not his looks are my soul's food?
Pity the dearth that I have pinèd in
By longing for that food so long a time.
Didst thou but know the inly touch of love
Thou wouldst as soon go kindle fire with snow
As seek to quench the fire of love with words.

[LUCETTA. I do not seek to quench your love's hot fire,
But qualify the fire's extreme rage,
Lest it should burn above the bounds of reason.]

The more thou damm'st it up, the more it burns.
The current that with gentle murmur glides,
Thou know'st, being stopp'd, impatiently doth rage.
But when his fair course is not hinderèd
He makes sweet music with th'enamell'd stones,
Giving a gentle kiss to every sedge
He overtaketh in his pilgrimage.
And so by many winding nooks he strays
With willing sport to the wild ocean.
Then let me go, and hinder not my course.
I'll be as patient as a gentle stream,
And make a pastime of each weary step
Till the last step have brought me to my love.
And there I'll rest as after much turmoil
A blessèd soul doth in Elysium. 〞

GLOSSARY

mean method
dearth famine
inly heartfelt
qualify modify, diminish
sedge reed
Elysium paradise

Richard III

William Shakespeare (1594)

WHO ☞   *Lady Anne, the young widow of the murdered Price of Wales, late 20s or older.*

WHERE ☞   *On the street, between St Paul's and Chertsey monastery, the place of burial.*

TO WHOM ☞   *The corpse of Henry VI and the bystanders.*

WHEN ☞   *1471.*

WHAT HAS JUST HAPPENED ☞   *Henry VI has been murdered, leaving Edward IV as king, though he is very sick. Richard, Duke of Gloucester is King Edward's brother, and is determined to seize power himself.*

This speech comes in the second scene of the play, during the funeral procession of Henry VI. Lady Anne asks the pallbearers to lay down the corpse of her father-in-law, that she might say her final goodbye. She knows Richard is responsible for his death and that of her late husband.

WHAT SHE WANTS/OBJECTIVES TO PLAY ☞

- *To give due rights to her beloved father-in-law, the late King.*
- *To curse Richard. She knows he is liable for all that has befallen the House of Lancaster, her family; she is raging on a private and almost domestic level.*
- *To publicly denounce Richard, a conscious political act in itself.*

Lady Anne

66 Set down, set down your honourable load,
If honour may be shrouded in a hearse,
Whilst I a while obsequiously lament
Th'untimely fall of virtuous Lancaster.

They set the coffin down.

Poor key-cold figure of a holy king!
Pale ashes of the House of Lancaster!
Thou bloodless remnant of that royal blood!
Be it lawful that I invocate thy ghost,
To hear the lamentations of poor Anne,
Wife to thy Edward, to thy slaughter'd son,
Stabb'd by the selfsame hand that made these wounds!
Lo, in these windows that let forth thy life,
I pour the helpless balm of my poor eyes.
O curs'd be the hand that made these holes!
Curs'd the blood that let this blood from hence!
Curs'd the heart that had the heart to do it!
More direful hap betide that hated wretch,
That makes us wretched by the death of thee,
Than I can wish to wolves, to spiders, toads,
Or any creeping venom'd thing that lives!
If ever he have child, abortive be it,
Prodigious, and untimely brought to light,
Whose ugly and unnatural aspect
May fright the hopeful mother at the view;
And that be heir to his unhappiness!
If ever he have wife, let her be made
More miserable by the death of him
Than I am made by my young lord and thee!
Come, now towards Chertsey with your holy load,
Taken from Paul's to be interr'd there.

The gentlemen lift the coffin.

And still, as you are weary of this weight,
Rest you, whiles I lament King Henry's corpse. **99**

GLOSSARY

obsequiously with devotion
helpless balm ineffective medicine
direful hap betide disastrous fortune visit
prodigious monstrous
aspect appearance

The Comedy of Errors

William Shakespeare (1595)

WHO ☞   *Adriana, wife of Antipholus of Ephesus, 20s.*

WHERE ☞   *A street in Ephesus.*

TO WHOM ☞   *To a man she believes to be her husband, in the presence of her sister Luciana.*

WHEN ☞   *Contemporary with authorship.*

WHAT HAS JUST HAPPENED ☞   *Adriana is a loving, but jealous wife, who is regularly put out by her husband's attentions to other women. The confusion and error at the centre of this play further fan the flames of this jealousy. In this scene she accosts whom she believes to be her husband, Antipholus, in the street, ordering him home to eat. The man is actually her husband's long-lost twin.*

WHAT SHE WANTS/OBJECTIVES TO PLAY ☞

- *To make him feel terrible about his lack of attention and her suspicion that he is seeing someone else.*

- *To return him to his former self, the man once so besotted with her, by both charming and berating him.*

- *To remind him they are married – they are one; well, she is his better half, and what he feels impacts on her directly.*

- *To warn him: if the tables were turned and it was she who was suspected of having an affair, he would be going crazy; he is getting off lightly.*

Adriana

❝ Ay, ay, Antipholus, look strange and frown:
Some other mistress hath thy sweet aspects.
I am not Adriana, nor thy wife.
The time was once when thou unurg'd wouldst vow
That never words were music to thine ear,

That never object pleasing in thine eye,
That never touch well welcome to thy hand,
That never meat sweet-savour'd in thy taste,
Unless I spake, or look'd, or touch'd, or carv'd to thee.
How comes it now, my husband, O how comes it
That thou art then estrangèd from thyself? –
Thy 'self' I call it, being strange to me
That, undividable, incorporate,
Am better than thy dear self's better part.
Ah, do not tear away thyself from me;
For know, my love, as easy mayst thou fall
A drop of water in the breaking gulf,
And take unmingled thence that drop again
Without addition or diminishing,
As take from me thyself, and not me too.
How dearly would it touch thee to the quick
Shouldst thou but hear I were licentious,
And that this body, consecrate to thee,
By ruffian lust should be contaminate?
Wouldst thou not spit at me, and spurn at me,
And hurl the name of husband in my face,
And tear the stain'd skin off my harlot brow,
And from my false hand cut the wedding ring,
And break it with a deep-divorcing vow?
I know thou canst, and therefore see thou do it!
I am possess'd with an adulterate blot;
My blood is mingled with the crime of lust.
For if we two be one, and thou play false,
I do digest the poison of thy flesh,
Being strumpeted by thy contagion.
Keep then fair league and truce with thy true bed,
I live unstain'd, thou undishonourèd. **99**

GLOSSARY

sweet-savour'd delicious
carv'd to carved meat for
incorporate combined in one body
fall let drop
licentious promiscuous
possess'd with endowed with

King John

William Shakespeare (1596)

WHO ☞ *Constance, Duchess of Brittany, mother of Arthur, mid-30s or more.*

WHERE ☞ *In King Philip's camp, after the Battle of Angiers, France.*

TO WHOM ☞ *King Philip and the Cardinal.*

WHEN ☞ *1201.*

WHAT HAS JUST HAPPENED ☞ *In her attempt to put her son Arthur on the throne of England, following his displacement by his uncle King John, Constance has aligned herself with King Philip of France. However, following an initial battle, England and France agree peace. But when King John is excommunicated from the Catholic Church, Pandulph, the Pope's legate, orders the French to resume their warfare upon King John. In the conflict that follows, John's army beats back the French and captures Arthur, taking him back to England. Constance has just been told this: she is hysterical and beyond comfort, as it indicates his sure and imminent torture and death. Largely unsympathetic, King Philip and Cardinal Pandulph accuse her of being 'as fond of grief as of your child' and suggest that she is demonstrating 'madness, and not sorrow'.*

WHAT SHE WANTS/OBJECTIVES TO PLAY ☞

- *To not live in a world that doesn't hold her son in it.*
- *To distance those she is with from her grief, and to belittle them as counsellors.*
- *To vent her agony and despair, she will rage – she is entitled to.*
- *To let the world know of the horror that has befallen her.*

Lady Constance

❝ No, I defy all counsel, all redress,
But that which ends all counsel, true redress:
Death, Death, O amiable, lovely Death,
Thou odoriferous stench: sound rottenness,
Arise forth from the couch of lasting night,
Thou hate and terror to prosperity,
And I will kiss thy detestable bones,
And put my eyeballs in thy vaulty brows,
And ring these fingers with thy household worms,
And stop this gap of breath with fulsome dust,
And be a carrion monster like thyself.
Come, grin on me, and I will think thou smil'st
And buss thee as thy wife: Misery's love,
O, come to me!

[KING PHILIP. O fair affliction, peace!]

No no, I will not, having breath to cry:
O that my tongue were in the thunder's mouth!
Then with a passion would I shake the world,
And rouse from sleep that fell anatomy
Which cannot hear a lady's feeble voice,
Which scorns a modern invocation.

[PANDULPH. Lady, you utter madness, and not sorrow.]

Thou art not holy to belie me so.
I am not mad: this hair I tear is mine,
My name is Constance, I was Geoffrey's wife,
Young Arthur is my son, and he is lost:
I am not mad – I would to God I were!
For then 'tis like I should forget myself.
O, if I could, what grief should I forget?
Preach some philosophy to make me mad,
And thou shalt be canonis'd, Cardinal.
For, being not mad, but sensible of grief,
My reasonable part produces reason
How I may be deliver'd of these woes,
And teaches me to kill or hang myself.

If I were mad, I should forget my son,
Or madly think a babe of clouts were he.
I am not mad. Too well, too well I feel
The different plague of each calamity. [. . .]

Grief fills the room up of my absent child,
Lies in his bed, walks up and down with me,
Puts on his pretty looks, repeats his words,
Remembers me of all his gracious parts,
Stuffs out his vacant garments with his form;
Then have I reason to be fond of grief.
Fare you well; had you such a loss as I,
I could give better comfort than you do.

   She unbinds her hair.

I will not keep this form upon my head,
When there is such disorder in my wit.
O Lord! My boy, my Arthur, my fair son!
My life, my joy, my food, my all the world!
My widow-comfort, and my sorrow's cure! 99

GLOSSARY

odoriferous sweet-smelling
couch bed
carrion scavenging (preying on rotten flesh)
buss kiss
fell anatomy dreadful skeleton
modern invocation trite appeal
belie slander
sensible of sensitive to
clouts swaddling clothes

Bussy D'Ambois

George Chapman (1604)

WHO ☞   *Tamyra, Countess of Montsurry. 20s plus.*

WHERE ☞   *In Tamyra's private chambers.*

TO WHOM ☞   *She believes she is alone after the line break, on dismissing her maidservant.*

WHEN ☞   *1580s.*

WHAT HAS JUST HAPPENED ☞   *Tamyra has just said goodbye to her husband, the Count. He will be back the following morning. We believe her to be chaste; in the previous scene she rebuffed the advances made on her by the King's brother, Monsieur. She pleaded a case for honour within marriage. When she complained of his advances, her husband suggested she just let it be: that was the way of the court. But we now learn that she is actually in love with somebody else, the eponymous hero of the play. She knows if she gives in to her desire for him, hell gates will open for her; she knows that everything is at stake, but she cannot resist him any longer. Bussy D'Ambois, her would-be lover, is an enchanting mix of poet and brutal war machine; he is newly returned to the court and very much flavour of the month. She is waiting for the Friar to bring him up to her chamber through a secret back vault.*

WHAT SHE WANTS/OBJECTIVES TO PLAY ☞

- *To win the natural world's approval for the sin she is about to commit, and to draw on its strength to give her the courage to see the liaison through.*

- *To abandon herself totally to this moment of longing: there will be no going back and she wants to go ahead with full awareness.*

Tamyra

" Farewell, my light and life. But not in him,
(In mine own dark love and light bent to another.)
Alas, that in the wane of our affections
We should supply it with a full dissembling,
In which each youngest maid is grown a mother.
Frailty is fruitful, one sin gets another:
Our loves like sparkles are, that brightest shine
When they go out; most vice shows most divine.
Go maid, to bed; lend me your book, I pray:
Not, like yourself, for form; I'll this night trouble
None of your services: make sure the doors,
And call your other fellows to their rest.

[PERO (*aside*). I will, yet I will watch to know why you watch.]

Now all the peaceful regents of the night,
Silently-gliding exhalations,
Languishing winds, and murmuring falls of waters,
Sadness of heart and ominous secureness,
Enchantments, dead sleeps, all the friends of rest,
That ever wrought upon the life of man,
Extend your utmost strengths, and this charm'd hour
Fix like the Centre! Make the violent wheels
Of Time and Fortune stand, and great Existence,
The Maker's treasury, now not seem to be,
To all but my approaching friends and me!
They come, alas, they come! Fear, fear and hope
Of one thing, at one instant, fight in me:
I love what most I loathe, and cannot live,
Unless I compass that which holds my death:
For love is hateful without love again,
And he I love, will loathe me, when he sees
I fly my sex, my virtue, my renown,
To run so madly on a man unknown.

The vault opens.

See, see, the gulf is opening that will swallow
Me and my fame for ever; I will in,
And cast myself off, as I ne'er had been. **99**

GLOSSARY

make sure secure
exhalations shooting stars
wrought upon practised charms on
the Centre the unmoving pivot of the universe
compass accomplish
I will in . . . ne'er been I will dive into oblivion

The Honest Whore

Thomas Dekker (1604)

WHO ☞   *Bellafront, an ex-prostitute.*

WHERE ☞   *In the home Bellafront shares with her husband Matheo.*

TO WHOM ☞   *Hippolyto, a gentleman: an old friend of Matheo.*

WHEN ☞   *Contemporary with authorship.*

WHAT HAS JUST HAPPENED ☞   *In the previous part of the play, Bellafront, the honest whore of the title, had undergone a moral conversion after being read the riot act by Hippolyto vis-à-vis prostitution. She became honest, and married Matheo, with whom she had slept while still a prostitute. But Matheo has snubbed Bellafront's marital devotion, and instead wants her to return to prostitution to earn money. So she has petitioned the happily married Hippolyto to act on her behalf and talk with Matheo. But far from being on her side, Hippolyto himself thinks it is not such a bad idea, with a mind to partaking of her wares himself. This is her response.*

WHAT SHE WANTS/OBJECTIVES TO PLAY ☞

- *To stoutly reject him and his advances, using much the same language that he used when rejecting her in the first part of the play.*

- *To drum some sense into him by lecturing him on the history of the woman's sexual lot in life.*

- *To remind him that once he has sated his appetite for the prostitute, she inevitably becomes worthless and devalued in his eyes.*

- *To belittle him: he is offering to dishonour her husband, and his friend's, bed.*

- *To put him on the spot with all his talk of how prostitution isn't necessarily a dishonourable way of life by asking why he doesn't suggest his wife take it up.*

- *To shame him by wiping the floor with him intellectually, morally and personally.*

Bellafront

❝ To prove a woman should not be a whore:
When she was made, she had one man and no more;
Yet she was tied to laws then, for, even then,
'Tis said, she was not made for men, but man.
Anon, t'increase earth's brood, the law was varied,
Men should take many wives, and though they married
According to that act, yet 'tis not known
But that those wives were only tied to one.
New parliaments were since: for now one woman
Is shar'd between three hundred – nay, she's common.
Common? As spotted leopards, whom for sport
Men hunt to get the flesh, but care not for't.
So spread they nets of gold and tune their calls
To enchant silly women to take falls,
Swearing they are angels, which that they may win
They'll hire the devil to come with false dice in.
Oh, Sirens' subtle tunes! Yourselves you flatter
And our weak sex betray. So men love water:
It serves to wash their hands but, being once foul,
The water down is pour'd, cast out of doors,
And even of such base use do men make whores.
A harlot, like a hen, more sweetness reaps
To pick men one by one up, than in heaps,
Yet all feeds but confounding. Say you should taste me:
I serve but for the time, and when the day
Of war is done, am cashier'd out of pay.
If like lame soldiers I could beg, that's all,
And there's lust's rendezvous: an hospital.
Who then would be a man's slave, a man's woman?
She's half-starv'd the first day that feeds in common.

[HIPPOLYTO. If all the threads of harlots' lives are spun
So coarse as you would make them, tell me why
You so long lov'd the trade?]

     If all the threads
Of harlots' lives be fine as you would make them,
Why do not you persuade your wife turn whore,
And all dames else to fall before that sin?
Like an ill husband (though I knew the same
To be my undoing) follow'd I that game.
Oh, when the work of lust had earn'd my bread,
To taste it, how I trembled, lest each bit,
Ere it went down, should choke me chewing it!
My bed seem'd like a cabin hung in hell,
The bawd hell's porter, and the lickerish wine
The pander fetch'd was like an easy fine,
For which methought I leas'd away my soul:
And oftentimes even in my quaffing bowl
Thus said I to myself: 'I am a whore
And have drunk down thus much confusion more' [. . .]

Why dote you on that which you did once detest?
I cannot (seeing she's woven of such bad stuff)
Set colours on a harlot base enough. **❞**

GLOSSARY

Sirens the legendary sea-demons whose beautiful songs lured sailors
  onto the rocks
all feeds but confounding only destruction is nourished
cashier'd out of pay discharged without payment
in common at the communal trough
lickerish inflammatory of lust
pander pimp, procurer
fine financial contract
quaffing bowl punch-bowl

The Dutch Courtesan

John Marston (1604)

WHO ☞　　　*Beatrice, a young lady, late teens / early 20s.*

WHERE ☞　　*At her window, early morning.*

TO WHOM ☞　*Her husband-to-be, Freevill.*

WHEN ☞　　 *Contemporary with authorship.*

WHAT HAS JUST HAPPENED ☞　*Freevill is sexually and emotionally involved with Franceschina, the 'Dutch Courtesan' of the title, but he is supposed to marry Beatrice, whom he is currently serenading. This is the first time we see Beatrice in the play. She is everything Franceschina is not in her demure nature and formality. And she is clearly devoted to him, blissfully oblivious to his compromised virtue.*

WHAT SHE WANTS/OBJECTIVES TO PLAY ☞

- *To respond appropriately and with all due respect to his singing his devotion to her at her window.*

- *To assure him that her love, though couched in far simpler terms than his for her, is its equal and that she is his.*

- *To make some deal with the offering of the ring that binds them in an entirely personal and informal way, as opposed to just reinforcing what is a formal engagement.*

- *To somewhat calm his ardour: his love is extreme, and she is by nature temperate.*

Beatrice

❝ Lov'd sir,
The honour of your wish return to you.
I cannot with a mistress' compliment,
Forcèd discourses, or nice art of wit
Give entertain to your dear wish'd presence;

But safely thus: what hearty gratefulness,
Unsullen silence, unaffected modesty,
And an unignorant shamefastness can express,
Receive as your protested due. Faith, my heart,
I am your servant.
O let not my secure simplicity
Breed your mislike, as one quite void of skill;
'Tis grace enough in us not to be ill.
I can some good, and, faith, I mean no hurt;
Do not, then, sweet, wrong sober ignorance.
I judge you all of virtue, and our vows
Should kill all fears that base distrust can move.
My soul, what say you? Still you love? [. . .]

Dear my loved heart, be not so passionate;
Nothing extreme lives long. [. . .]

I give you faith; and, prithee, since,
Poor soul, I am so easy to believe thee,
Make it much more pity to deceive me.
Wear this slight favour in my remembrance. 〝

GLOSSARY

nice art of wit sophisticated intellectual expression
unignorant shamefastness knowing modesty
your protested due the due qualities I protest are yours
secure trusting
ill wicked
I can I am able to do
all of virtue entirely virtuous

The Dutch Courtesan

John Marston (1604)

WHO ☞ *Crispinella, plain-speaking daughter of Sir Hubert Subboys and sister to the refined, virtuous and modest Beatrice. 20s.*

WHERE ☞ *In the sisters' family home.*

TO WHOM ☞ *Talking in private with her sister Beatrice, who is betrothed to Freevill. Their nanny is also present.*

WHEN ☞ *Contemporary with authorship.*

WHAT HAS JUST HAPPENED ☞ *The sisters are quite different from each other. Crispinella is tired of hearing her infatuated sister droning on about her husband-to-be, Freevill, who has recently sent a sonnet written by him in honour of Beatrice's kiss. Beatrice has been reciting it. Crispinella is direct in her speech, and she finds Freevill's influence on her sister, though she does largely approve of him, just too much to bear.*

WHAT SHE WANTS/OBJECTIVES TO PLAY ☞

- *To provoke her sister out of the dewy-eyed misty stage of being in love, and to bring her rudely up to measure with the reality of it all.*

- *To undermine Beatrice, and to have a good laugh at her expense, though not in a cruel way.*

- *To alert her virginal sister to what lies in store – imagine a rather brusque sex education class!*

- *To assert her plain-speaking, speak-as-I-find nature as a virtue, free from hypocrisy and prissiness and in stark contrast to what her sister perceives of as 'normal'.*

Crispinella

❝ Pish, sister Beatrice! Prithee read no more; my stomach o'late stands against kissing extremely.

[BEATRICE. Why, good Crispinella?]

By the faith and trust I bear to my face, 'tis grown one of the most unsavoury ceremonies. Body o'beauty! 'tis one of the most unpleasing, injurious customs to ladies. Any fellow that has but one nose on his face, and standing-collar and skirts also lined with taffety sarcenet, must salute us on the lips as familiarly – Soft skins save us! There was a stub-bearded John-a-Stile with a ployden's face saluted me last day and struck his bristles through my lips. I ha' spent ten shillings in pomatum since to skin them again! Marry, if a nobleman or a knight with one lock visit us, though his unclean goose-turd-green teeth ha' the palsy, his nostrils smell worse than a putrefied marrowbone, and his loose beard drops into our bosom, yet we must kiss him with a cur'sy. A curse! For my part, I had as lief they would break wind in my lips.

[BEATRICE. Fie, Crispinella! You speak too broad.]

No jot, sister. Let's ne'er be ashamed to speak what we be not ashamed to think. I dare as boldly speak venery as think venery.

[BEATRICE. Faith sister, I'll be gone if you speak so broad.]

Will you so? No basfulness seize you! We pronounce boldly robbery, murder, treason, which deeds must needs be far more loathsome than an act which is so natural, just, and necessary as that of procreation. You shall have an hypocritical vestal virgin speak that with close teeth publicly which she will receive with open mouth privately. For my own part, I consider nature without apparel; without disguising of custom or compliment, I give thoughts words, and words truth, and truth boldness. She whose honest freeness makes it her virtue to speak what she thinks, will make it her necessity to think what is good. I love no prohibited things, and yet I would have nothing prohibited by policy, but by virtue; for, as in the fashion of the time, those books that are called in are most in sale and request, so in nature those actions that are most prohibited are most desired.

[BEATRICE. Good, quick sister, stay your pace. We are private, but the world would censure you; for truly, severe modesty is women's virtue.]

Fie, fie! Virtue is a free, pleasant, buxom quality. I love a constant countenance well; but this forward, ignorant coyness, sour, austere, lumpish, uncivil privateness, that promises nothing but rough skins and hard stools – ha! Fie o't! Good for nothing but for nothing. – Well, nurse, and what do you conceive of all this? 🗨

GLOSSARY

standing-collar fashionably starched lace collar
taffety sarcenet fine silk
John-a-Stile with a ployden's face Mr So-and-so with the face of a
    lawyer
pomatum face lotion
skin restore skin to
palsy disease
with a cur'sey politely, deferentially
too broad too vulgarly
venery sex
vestal virgin maidens of chastity
called in censored, banned
lumpish dull of spirit

A Mad World, My Masters

Thomas Middleton (1605)

WHO ☞   *'Mother'. Mother to prostitute Frances Gullman, and also her pimp. 30s plus. A woman of the world.*

WHERE ☞   *In a London street.*

TO WHOM ☞   *Her daughter.*

WHEN ☞   *Contemporary with authorship.*

WHAT HAS JUST HAPPENED ☞   *Frances is as colourful a character as her mother. She is the sole mistress of the wealthy – and very old – Sir Bounteous Progress. As Mother hands Frances a gift from Sir Bounteous, we learn he is only one of many suitors. Her mother is feeling insecure about her daughter's flightiness; she wants her to settle down and knows that Sir Bounteous, despite his assurances, is never going to propose.*

WHAT SHE WANTS/OBJECTIVES TO PLAY ☞

- *To persuade her daughter to marry the next gullible, wealthy man.*

- *To warn her daughter that she is running out of tricks as regards selling her daughter's 'virginity' – which she has sold 15 times now. Making business is getting harder, the older Frances gets.*

- *To warn her daughter they are living in times when the world and even its dullest inhabitants are getting smarter.*

- *To remind her daughter that marriage and the respected title of wife will help, not hinder, her trade as a prostitute – 'a virtuous name may sin at pleasure, and ne'er think of shame'.*

Mother

❝ Every part of the world shoots up daily into more subtlety. The very spider weaves her cauls with more art and

cunning to entrap the fly.
The shallow ploughman can distinguish now
'Twixt simple truth and a dissembling brow.
Your base mechanic fellow can spy out
A weakness in a lord, and learns to flout.
How does't behove us then, that live by sleight,
To have our wits wound up to their stretch'd height?

Fifteen times thou know'st I have sold thy maidenhead to make
up a dowry for thy marriage: and yet there's maidenhead
enough for old Sir Bounteous still. He'll be all his lifetime
about it yet, and be as far to seek when he has done.

The sums that I have told upon thy pillow!
I shall once see those golden days again.
Though fifteen, all thy maidenheads are not gone:
The Italian is not serv'd yet, nor the French;
The British men come for a dozen at once,
They engross all the market. Tut, my girl,
'Tis nothing but a politic conveyance,
A sincere carriage, a religious eyebrow,
That throws their charms over the worldlings' senses;
And when thou spiest a fool that truly pities
The false springs of thine eyes,
And honourably dotes upon thy love,
If he be rich, set him by for a husband.
Be wisely temper'd and learn this, my wench:
Who gets th' opinion for a virtuous name
May sin at pleasure, and ne'er think of shame. **99**

GLOSSARY

cauls pieces of lacework
mechanic menial handicraftsman
flout abandon deference
sleight cunning
told counted
engross glut
politic conveyance deft dexterity
charms spells
worldlings lowly inhabitants of the world
gets th'opinion for a virtuous name establishes a virtuous reputation

The Devil's Charter

Barnabe Barnes (1607)

WHO ☞　　　*Lucretia Borgia, daughter of Pope Alexander VI, sister to Cardinal Cesare Borgia and the Duke of Candy. 20s.*

WHERE ☞　　*In her dressing room.*

TO WHOM ☞　*To herself in the mirror and to her servant Motticilla.*

WHEN ☞　　*Around 1500.*

WHAT HAS JUST HAPPENED ☞　*Lucretia is about to be murdered with poisoned make-up, by order of her father, the Pope, with whom she has been conducting an incestuous affair. Alexander only became Pope by making a deal with the Devil (the Charter of the title), signing away his soul – which sets the tone for this barbaric world of the murderous Borgias. Lucretia herself killed her own good husband, Gismond, then made it look like a suicide. She is preparing for an evening out and comes in holding a small bottle of precious cosmetic, a gift from a king.*

WHAT SHE WANTS/OBJECTIVES TO PLAY ☞

- *To get into the spirit of the evening to come.*
- *To relive some of the admiring praise lavished on her in the past from would-be lovers.*
- *To intoxicate herself with self-admiration.*

Lucretia

❝ Kind Lodowick, hadst thou presented me
With Persian clothes of gold or tinselry,
With rich Arabian odours, precious stones,
Or what brave women hold in highest price,
Could not have been so gracious as this tincture
Which I more value than my richest jewels.

Oh, Motticilla!

Enter Motticilla.

Bring me some mixtures and my dressing boxes.
This night I purpose privately to sup
With my Lord Cardinal of Capua.

*Enter pages with a table, two looking glasses, a box with
combs and instruments, and a rich bowl.*

Bring me some blanching-water in this bowl.

Exit Motticilla. She looketh in her glass.

Here I perceive a little rivelling
Above my forehead; but I wimple it
Either with jewels or a lock of hair,
And yet it is as white as the pure snow.
Oh God, when that sweet Marquis Mantova
Did in Ferrara feast my lord and me,
What rich comparisons and similes
He with ingenious fantasy devis'd,
Doting upon the whiteness of my brows!
As that 'Betwixt them stood the chair of state,
Compos'd of ivory for the Paphian Queen,
Sitting in comfort after amorous conquest,'
And kiss'd my forehead twenty thousand times.
Oft have I wish'd the colour of this hair
More bright and not of such a Spanish dye,
And yet the Duke of Bourbon, on his knees,
As the divinest favour of this world,
Did beg one lock to make a bracelet,
For which few hairs, he garnishèd my head
With jewels worth six thousand crowns at least.
My beaming eyes, yet full of majesty,
Dart love and give bright lustre to the glass,
As when the sunbeams touch a diamond.
The Prince of Salerne solemnly did swear
These eyes were quivers which such shafts did bear
That were so sharp, and had such fiery touch,
As Cupid's arrows never had so much.

The rosy garden of these amorous cheeks;
My nose, the gracious fort of conquering love,
Breathing attractive odours to those lovers
That languish and are vanquish'd with desire.
Gonzago calleth it 'the silver perch,
Where Venus' turtles mutual pleasure search'.
Sweet mouth, the ruby port to paradise
Of my world's pleasure, from whence issue forth
Many false brags, bold sallies, sweet supplies;
A chin, the matchless fabric of fair nature;
A neck; two breasts upon whose cherry nipples
So many sweet solutions Cupid suck'd.

Enter Motticilla with the water

Give me some blanching-water in this bowl.
Wash my face, Motticilla, with this cloth.
So, 'tis well. Now will I try these colours.
Give me that oil of talc,
Take sarc'net, Motticilla, smooth my forehead. 〞

GLOSSARY

tinselry glittering work
brave proud
tincture blusher, 'rouge'
blanching water cleansing lotion
rivelling wrinkling
wimple disguise (as with a nun's headgear)
Paphian Queen Venus, the goddess of love
turtles turtle-doves
sarc'net fine silk

The Winter's Tale

William Shakespeare (1610)

WHO ☞　　　*Hermione, Queen of Sicilia. Late 20s plus.*

WHERE ☞　　*In an open court.*

TO WHOM ☞　*The judge, her husband, the King.*

WHEN ☞　　*In a pre-Christian, mythical time.*

WHAT HAS JUST HAPPENED ☞　*When Leontes fails to persuade his friend to extend his stay in Sicily, he asks his wife, Hermione, to try. She does so, and Leontes irrationally suspects that they are lovers. He accuses her of adultery and treason, sends her to prison, and bars her from seeing her son. In prison she gives birth to a girl, who is brought to Leontes in the hope of softening him, but he denies paternity and orders her to be exposed to the elements and left to die. Hermione is brought to trial; Leontes acts as both judge and juror. She pleads not guilty.*

WHAT SHE WANTS/OBJECTIVES TO PLAY ☞

- *To assert her innocence.*
- *To shame her husband with her protestations – she does not fear death as her life is so unbearable.*
- *To honour and respect her King, while maintaining her dignity, majesty and propriety.*

Hermione

❝ Since what I am to say must be but that
Which contradicts my accusation, and
The testimony on my part no other
But what comes from myself, it shall scarce boot me
To say 'Not Guilty'. Mine integrity
Being counted falsehood shall, as I express it,
Be so receiv'd. But thus: if powers divine
Behold our human actions – as they do –
I doubt not then but innocence shall make

False accusation blush, and tyranny
Tremble at patience. You, my lord, best know –
Who least will seem to do so – my past life
Hath been as continent, as chaste, as true
As I am now unhappy; which is more
Than history can pattern, though devis'd
And play'd to take spectators. [. . .]
Sir, spare your threats:
The bug which you would fright me with, I seek.
To me can life be no commodity;
The crown and comfort of my life, your favour,
I do give lost, for I do feel it gone,
But know not how it went. My second joy,
And first-fruits of my body, from his presence
I am barr'd, like one infectious. My third comfort
(Starr'd most unluckily) is from my breast
(The innocent milk in it most innocent mouth)
Hal'd out to murder; myself on every post
Proclaim'd a strumpet, with immodest hatred
The child-bed privilege denied, which 'longs
To women of all fashion; lastly, hurried
Here, to this place, i'th' open air, before
I have got strength of limit. Now, my liege,
Tell me what blessings I have here alive,
That I should fear to die? Therefore proceed.
But yet hear this: mistake me not: no life,
I prize it not a straw, but for mine honour,
Which I would free: if I shall be condemn'd
Upon surmises, all proofs sleeping else
But what your jealousies awake, I tell you
'Tis rigour and not law. Your honours all,
I do refer me to the Oracle:
Apollo be my judge! **99**

GLOSSARY

continent temperate, restrained, chaste
more than history can pattern more than can be expressed in words
the child-bed privilege denied deprived of the rights earned by a mother
   in labour

The Tamer Tamed

John Fletcher (1611)

WHO ☞ *Maria, 20s/early 30s, wife of a few hours to Petruchio. He was married to her recently deceased cousin Kate – better known as the couple at the heart of Shakespeare's* The Taming of the Shrew.

WHERE ☞ *Outdoors, near to the church where she was lately married to Petruchio.*

TO WHOM ☞ *Her sister Livia and cousin Bianca.*

WHEN ☞ *Contemporary with authorship.*

WHAT HAS JUST HAPPENED ☞ *Maria has just married Petruchio. The talk is of a lamb to the slaughter, but Maria has come away from the church with other things on her mind than following her husband's will sheepishly! An adventurous side to her is revealed. She wants to tame the man who attempted – allegedly successfully – to tame, even break, her spirited and beautiful cousin Kate. Her sister has just suggested that she take herself off with 'obedient hands' to the marital bed.*

WHAT SHE WANTS/OBJECTIVES TO PLAY ☞

- *To impress upon her sister, who is promised to a much older man whom she doesn't love, that you can be a wife and hold all the power – even to the point of being able to cuckold him with her younger true love.*

- *To teach her sister that this behaviour is not capriciousness on her part: that she is sick of weak women.*

- *To impress upon the women that any wife who does not behave as a woman and a person in her own right, is nothing more than an animal.*

- *To awaken an awareness of the very real power within them.*

- *To shock them out of subservience.*

- *To encourage them to play the husbands at their own game.*

- *This text is taken from the RSC adapted edition of the play, published by Nick Hern Books. Omissions from the text are indicated by [. . .].*

Maria

66 To bed? No, Livia, there are comets hang
Prodigious over that yet. Ne'er start, wench.
Before I know that heat, there's a fellow must
Be made a man, for yet he is a monster;
Here must his head be, Livia.

[LIVIA.   Never hope it.
'Tis as easy with a sieve to scoop the ocean as
To tame Petruchio.]

                    Stay, Lucina hear me,
Never unlock the treasure of my womb: if I do
Give way unto my married husband's will,
Or be a wife in anything but hopes,
Till I have made him easy as a child,
And tame as fear.
And when I kiss him, till I have my will,
May I be barren of delights, and know
Only what pleasures are in dreams and guesses! [. . .]
And I'll do it bravely
Or may I knit my life out ever after.

[LIVIA. In what part of the world got she this spirit?
Yet pray, Maria, look before you truly
Besides the disobedience of a wife,
So distant from your sweetness –]

                    Disobedience?
You talk too tamely. By the faith I have
In mine own noble will, that childish woman
That lives a prisoner to her husband's pleasure
Has lost her making, and becomes a beast,
Created for his use, not fellowship. [. . .]
I have a new dance for him, and a mad one. [. . .]

Now thou com'st near the nature of a woman.
Hang these tame-hearted eyasses, that no sooner
See the lure out, and hear their husbands' holla,
But cry like kites upon 'em! The free haggard
(Which is that woman that hath wing and knows it,
Spirit and plume) will make an hundred checks
To show her freedom, sail in ev'ry air,
And look out ev'ry pleasure, not regarding
Lure nor quarry till her pitch command
What she desires, making her founder'd keeper
Be glad to fling out trains, and golden ones,
To take her down again. [. . .]
I'll tell thee, Livia, had this fellow tir'd
As many wives as horses under him
With spurring of their patience; had he got
A patent, with an office to reclaim us
Confirm'd by Parliament; had he all the malice
And subtlety of devils, or of us women,
Or anything that's worse than both – [. . .]
Or could he
Cast his wives new again, like bells, to make 'em
Sound to his will; or had the fearful name
Of the first breaker of wild women: yet
Yet would I undertake this man,
Turn him and bend him as I list, and mould him
Into a babe again, that aged women,
Wanting both teeth and spleen, may master him. 99

GLOSSARY

Lucina the Roman goddess of childbirth
bravely daringly
Or may I knit my life out ever after Or may I spend the rest of my life
    knitting
eyasses fledgling hawks
lure the bait used by falconers in training their birds
kites ignoble birds of prey
haggard wild hawk
checks swoops
trains decoys
list please
spleen passion

The Custom of the Country

John Fletcher (1619)

WHO ☞ *Guiomar, 40s. Sister to the Governor of Lisbon and mother to the dissolute Duarte – whom she believes to be dead, killed by Rutillio.*

WHERE ☞ *Guiomar's quarters in Lisbon.*

TO WHOM ☞ *Rutillio, an Italian, who loves Guiomar. In the presence of officers.*

WHEN ☞ *Contemporary with authorship.*

WHAT HAS JUST HAPPENED ☞ *Guiomar originally took Rutillio in and harboured him after she believed he had killed a man. She was very much in love with him. But when she discovered the man in question was her only son, Duarte, she banished him. After his arrest for this crime, Rutillio was bailed by a female pimp on condition that he work for her as a male prostitute, a fate he was rescued from by Duarte, whom he had not in fact killed at all and who is now a reformed character thanks to his 'near death' experience. Duarte is determined to put everything right, starting with the love he knows exists between his mother and Rutillio. He arranges, incognito, for a reconciliation. She has agreed to meet to consider Rutillio's proposal of marriage; it is actually a trap to have him re-arrested for her son's death.*

WHAT SHE WANTS/OBJECTIVES TO PLAY ☞

- *To make Rutillio suffer as she has suffered.*
- *To ridicule him, to make him feel small. Her heart was broken by a man she loved totally – and she is outraged that he should come seeking her out again, having been sent away.*
- *She wants to vent all her pent-up rage, her hurt and sense of betrayal, and to move on.*

Guiomar

" You are deceiv'd, sir.
You come besotted to your own destruction.
I sent not for you. What honour can ye add to me,
That brake that staff of honour my age lean'd on?
That robb'd me of that right made me a mother?
Hear me, thou wretched man, hear me with terror,
And let thine own bold folly shake thy soul.
Hear me pronounce thy death, that now hangs o'er thee,
Thou desperate fool. Who bade thee seek this ruin?
What mad, unmanly fate made thee discover
Thy curs'd face to me again? Was't not enough
To have the fair protection of my house
When misery and justice close pursued thee?
When thine own bloody sword cried out against thee,
Hatch'd in the life of him? Yet I forgave thee.
My hospitable word, even when I saw
The goodliest branch of all my blood lopp'd from me,
Did I not seal still to thee?

[RUTILIO.   I am gone.]

And when thou went'st, to imp thy misery
Did I not give thee means? But hark, ungrateful,
Was it not thus? To hide thy face and fly me?
To keep thy name forever from my memory,
Thy cursèd blood and kindred? Did I not swear then,
If ever (in this wretched life thou hast left me,
Short and unfortunate) I saw thee again,
Or came but to the knowledge where thou wander'dst,
To call my vow back and pursue with vengeance,
With all the miseries a mother suffers?

[RUTILLIO. I was born to be hang'd, there's no avoiding it.]

And dar'st thou with this impudence appear?
Walk like the winding sheet my son was put in,
Stain'd with those wounds? **"**

GLOSSARY

imp replenish (as feathers to a wing)
winding sheet shroud

The Custom of the Country

John Fletcher (1619)

WHO ☞   *Hippolyta, a 'rich and beautiful lady'. 20s plus.*

WHERE ☞   *In her private quarters in Lisbon.*

TO WHOM ☞   *Herself, in the presence of her servants.*

WHEN ☞   *Contemporary with the authorship.*

WHAT HAS JUST HAPPENED ☞ *She has fallen in love at first sight with Arnoldo, an Italian, washed up on the shores of Portugal. The love is both inexplicable and total on her part. She arranged for him to be brought to her chambers, where she tries to seduce him with food and gifts of jewels. He declined and fled. At the start of this speech she is beside herself, in agony. The break in the speech indicates where her servant tells her Arnoldo has been captured. According to her instructions, he has been accused of stealing her jewels and the governor has ordered his execution. She wrestles with what she should do next.*

WHAT SHE WANTS/OBJECTIVES TO PLAY ☞

- *To make herself feel better about the situation.*

- *To vent her outrage at what has happened.*

- *To make sense of the extraordinary behaviour on his part.*

  On the news of Arnoldo's capture, she wants:

- *To work out the rights and wrongs of her bringing about his death because he won't have her.*

- *To do the right thing – her honour and higher self win the day as she rushes off to save him.*

Hippolyta

❝ To be forc'd to woo,
Being a woman, could not but torment me;
But bringing for my advocates youth and beauty,

Set off with wealth – and then to be denied too,
Does comprehend all tortures. They flatter'd me
That said my looks were charms, my touches fetters,
My locks soft chains to bind the arms of princes
And make them in that wish'd-for bondage happy.
I am like others of a coarser feature,
As weak to allure, but in my dotage stronger.
I am no Circe; he, more than Ulysses,
Scorns all my offer'd bounties, slights my favours,
And, as I were some new Egyptian, flies me,
Leaving no pawn but my own shame behind him.
But he shall find that in my fell revenge
I am a woman, one that never pardons
The rude contemner of her proffer'd sweetness. [. . .]
Is that the means to quench the scorching heat
Of my enrag'd desires? Must innocence suffer
'Cause I am faulty? Or is my love so fatal
That of necessity it must destroy
The object it most longs for? Dull Hippolyta,
To think that injuries could make way for love
When courtesies were despis'd; that by his death
Thou shouldst gain that which only thou canst hope for
While he is living. My honour's at the stake now,
And cannot be preserv'd unless he perish.
The enjoying of the thing I love I ever
Have priz'd above my fame: why doubt I now, then?
One only way is left me to redeem all. –
Make ready my caroche. 〟

GLOSSARY

comprehend incorporate
Circe pronounced 'sursee', the legendary sorceress who bewitched . . .
Ulysses (*alias* Odysseus), whose crew washed up on her shores
Egyptian i.e. Queen Dido of Carthage, abandoned by Aeneas
dull dim, obtuse, stupid
caroche coach

The Changeling

Thomas Middleton and William Rowley (1622)

WHO ☞ *Beatrice, daughter of the Governor of the Castle of Alicante, Spain.*

WHERE ☞ *In her new husband's bedchamber.*

TO WHOM ☞ *Herself and the audience; it is a soliloquy but much of it is discovery as well as communication.*

WHEN ☞ *Contemporary with authorship.*

WHAT HAS JUST HAPPENED ☞ *Beatrice was betrothed initially to Alonso, but fell deeply in love with the nobleman Alsemero. In desperation she hired her father's servant DeFlores, a man she finds physically repulsive, to kill Alonso. The deal was she would offer her virginity to him as payment, or he would reveal her to be complicit in the murder. She had no option but to submit. Today she has married Alsemero but she is dreading the wedding night, not least because of what she finds when looking around his closet whilst he is out.*

WHAT SHE WANTS/OBJECTIVES TO PLAY ☞

- *To berate herself for being 'undone'.*
- *To let the audience know of her genuine distress, and her fears of being discovered. She had no idea he had all these potions to detect virginity. She was feeling terrible enough before discovering the closet, and afterwards feels desperate.*

Beatrice

❝ This fellow has undone me endlessly:
Never was bride so fearfully distress'd.
The more I think upon th' ensuing night,
And whom I am to cope with in embraces –
One that's ennobled both in blood and mind,
So clear in understanding (that's my plague now),

Before whose judgement will my fault appear
Like malefactors' crimes before tribunals
(There is no hiding on't) – the more I dive
Into my own distress. How a wise man
Stands for a great calamity! There's no venturing
Into his bed, what course soe'er I light upon,
Without my shame, which may grow up to danger.
He cannot but in justice strangle me
As I lie by him, as a cheater use me;
'Tis a precious craft to play with a false die
Before a cunning gamester. Here's his closet,
The key left in't, and he abroad i' th' park;
Sure 'twas forgot, I'll be so bold as look in't.

Opens closet.

Bless me! A right physician's closet 'tis,
Set round with vials, every one her mark too.
Sure he does practise physic for his own use,
Which may be safely call'd your great man's wisdom.
What manuscript lies here? 'The Book of Experiment,
Call'd Secrets in Nature'; so 'tis, 'tis so;
'How to know whether a woman be with child or no'.
I hope I am not yet; if he should try though!
Let me see – folio forty-five. Here 'tis;
The leaf tucked down upon't, the place suspicious.
'If you would know whether a woman be with child or not,
give her two spoonfuls of the white water in the glass C –'
Where's that glass C? Oh yonder I see it now,
'And if she be with child, she sleeps full twelve hours after,
if not, not.'
None of that water comes into my belly.
I'll know you from a hundred; I could break you now,
Or turn you into milk, and so beguile
The master of the mystery, but I'll look to you.
Ha! That which is next is ten times worse:
'How to know whether a woman be a maid or not'.
If that should be applied, what would become of me?
Belike he has a strong faith of my purity,
That never yet made proof; but this he calls

'A merry sleight, but true experiment, the author Antonius
Mizaldus. Give the party you suspect the quantity of a
spoonful of the water in the glass M, which upon her that is
a maid makes three several effects: 'twill make her
incontinently gape, then fall into a sudden sneezing, last into
a violent laughing; else dull, heavy, and lumpish.'
Where had I been?
I fear it, yet 'tis several hours to bedtime. **99**

GLOSSARY

fellow (1) base knave; (2) partner
cope with (1) fight with; (2) copulate with
stands for represents
die a single dice
right true
vials small flasks
physic medicine
folio page
belike probably
made proof successfully tested
sleight trick
incontinently gape stare, as if paralysed
lumpish dull of spirit

The Devil's Law-Case

John Webster (1623)

WHO ☞   *Leonora, mother of Romelio and Jolenta.*
Late 30s/40.

WHERE ☞   *In Leonora's home, Naples.*

TO WHOM ☞   *The audience: it is a soliloquy.*

WHEN ☞   *Contemporary with authorship.*

WHAT HAS JUST HAPPENED ☞   *Contarino had been near fatally wounded in a duel – he was fighting for the right to marry Jolenta, who had been set up to marry his rival, Ercole, by her brother Romelio and her mother Leonora. Romelio had gone to tend Contarino on his sick bed, prompted to bring him back to health by Leonora, but learning that the wealthy Contarino had left a will leaving everything to Jolenta should he die, he changes tack to hasten his end, by stabbing him to death. He has just told Leonora of the murder. But what was unknown by anyone was that Leonora was deeply in love with Contarino. She had supported the Ercole match expressly to free Contarino for her own use. Deluded, she had believed that the love was mutual, if unvoiced, and it would flower after Jolenta's marriage to another.*

WHAT SHE WANTS/OBJECTIVES TO PLAY ☞

- *To voice her horror at this turn of events: the sending of her own son to tend to Contarino, leading directly to his murder.*

- *To not live any longer in this world.*

- *To express, for the first time aloud, the sheer depth of her love for him and the logic of this love for a much younger man, to get the audience to understand the simplicity and purity of real love that overrides all barriers.*

- *To torment herself with recriminations.*

- *To denounce Romelio as a son, he is nothing to her now. Her hatred of him is warrior-like as she draws inspiration from the female Amazonians who would remove a breast in order to draw a bow across their chest more efficiently and so shoot more accurately.*

Leonora

❝ Never was woe like mine: O that my care
And absolute study to preserve his life,
Should be his absolute ruin! Is he gone then?
There is no plague i'th'world can be compar'd
To impossible desire, for they are plagued
In the desire itself: never, O never
Shall I behold him living, in whose life
I liv'd far sweetlier than in mine own.
A precise curiosity has undone me: why did I not
Make my love known directly? 'T had not been
Beyond example, for a matron to affect
I'th'honourable way of marriage,
So youthful a person. O I shall run mad:
For as we love our youngest children best,
So the last fruit of our affection,
Wherever we bestow it, is most strong,
Most violent, most unresistible,
Since 'tis indeed our latest harvest-home,
Last merriment 'fore winter. And we widows,
As men report of our best picture makers,
We love the piece we are in hand with better
Than all the excellent work we have done before:
And my son has depriv'd me of all this. Ha, my son!
I'll be a fury to him; like an Amazon lady,
I'd cut off this right pap, that gave him suck,
To shoot him dead. I'll no more tender him,
Than had a wolf stol'n to my teat i' th' night,
And robb'd me of my milk: nay, such a creature
I should love better far. – Ha, ha, what say you?
I do talk to somewhat, methinks: it may be
My evil genius. Do not the bells ring?
I have a strange noise in my head. O, fly in pieces!

Come age, and wither me into the malice
Of those that have been happy; let me have
One more property more than the Devil of Hell,
Let me envy the pleasure of youth heartily,
Let me in this life fear no kind of ill,
That have no good to hope for: let me die
In the distraction of that worthy princess,
Who loathèd food, and sleep, and ceremony,
For thought of losing that brave gentleman,
She would fain have sav'd, had not a false conveyance
Express'd him stubborn-hearted. Let me sink
Where neither man, nor memory may ever find me. **"**

GLOSSARY

precise curiosity over-elaborate scrupulousness
last merriment 'fore winter final fling before old age
in hand with currently working on
conveyance communication

A New Way to Pay Old Debts

Philip Massinger (1625)

WHO ☞   *Lady Alworth. A rich middle-aged widow. 40s.*

WHERE ☞   *Lady Alworth's home, in the North of England.*

TO WHOM ☞   *Lovell, an English Lord.*

WHEN ☞   *Contemporary with authorship.*

WHAT HAS JUST HAPPENED ☞   *Lovell has decided to marry Margaret, the beautiful daughter of the overt social climber, Sir Giles Overreach. Or so everyone thinks. Actually he and Margaret have agreed to string everyone along, not least to allow her relationship with Alworth, the stepson of Lady Alworth, to develop. Alworth has been acting as 'go-between'. Here, Lady Alworth, who has been supporting her stepson in his chosen love match, is trying to show Lovell that it is not appropriate for him to marry Margaret. Not least because her father, Overreach, has just been exposed as a money-grabbing fraud. Also, she rather likes Lovell herself. But Lovell thought Lady Alworth was being wooed, and had accepted Welborne's advances. She has not – and puts him right on that point. Welborne, a 'prodigal', is cut of the same cloth as Overreach and has been chancing it pursuing her. (Overreach, persuaded of a potential 'match' between Welborne and the Lady, has told Welborne that he can secure her lands for him, and she has found this out).*

WHAT SHE WANTS/OBJECTIVES TO PLAY ☞

- *To get him to release Margaret from the engagement.*

- *To reveal her respect and liking for him, so their courtship might have a chance to begin.*

- *To impress him linguistically, intellectually and as an equal.*

- *To remind Lovell that he is a member of the aristocracy – like herself – and does not come from 'new money' in the vulgar way that those like Sir Giles Overreach do.*

Lady Alworth

66 Now my good lord; if I may use my freedom,
As to an honour'd friend –

[LOVELL.   You lessen else
Your favour to me.]

                    I dare then say thus:
As you are noble (howe'er common men
Make sordid wealth the object and sole end
Of their industrious aims), 'twill not agree
With those of eminent blood (who are engag'd
More to prefer their honours than to increase
The state left to 'em by their ancestors)
To study large additions in their fortunes
And quite neglect their births: though I must grant
Riches well got to be a useful servant,
But a bad master.

[LOVELL   Madam, 'tis confess'd;
But what infer you from it?]

                    This, my lord,
That as all wrongs, though thrust into one scale
Slide of themselves off when right fills the other,
And cannot bide the trial: so all wealth
(I mean if ill acquired), cemented to honour
By virtuous ways achiev'd, and bravely purchas'd,
Is but as rubbish pour'd into a river
(Howe'er intended to make good the bank),
Rend'ring the water that was pure before,
Polluted, and unwholesome. I allow
The heir of St Giles Overreach, Margaret,
A maid well qualified, and the richest match
Our north part can make boast of: yet she cannot
With all that she brings with her fill their mouths,
That never will forget who was her father;
Or that my husband Alworth's lands, and Welborne's
(How wrung from both needs now no repetition)
Were real motive, that more work'd your lordship

To join your families, than her form, and virtues;
You may conceive the rest. 〞

state estate
grant concede
thrust into one scale loaded onto one side of a set of scales
allow concede
conceive readily supply

French and Spanish Golden Age

The golden era of Elizabethan and Jacobean drama was matched by a similarly rich Golden Age on the continent.

Spain was a country only recently defeated in war – and this had a notable effect on the writing of the time. It was nationalistic, principled and preoccupied with conduct, morality and integrity.

In Catholic France, actors were social outcasts, even denied a Christian burial. But its accomplishments between 1630 and 1680 lifted French theatre to an unrivalled pre-eminence in Europe, and kept it there throughout the eighteenth century. The comedies deal broadly with urban hypocrisy and small-time domestic villainy, drawing from the physical comedy and stereotypes of the *Commedia dell'Arte*. Rather than provoking belly laughs, these comedies, especially Molière's, are described by one contemporary critic as *'rire dans l'âme'* – or laughter in the soul.

The tragedies also deal with archetypes but on a grander scale, with the epic and timeless issues that underpin the very lives and aspirations of the pre-Republic French: honour, truth and faithfulness to the ruler. Many of the plots go back to Greek drama for inspiration, and the genre is truly neo-classical in its aspiration. Unlike Molière's verse, Racine's is lofty, grand and morally elevating, in both tone and form.

Like much of the English work, this period of European writing was characterised by a particularly vivid – almost physical – lyricism, a poetic language. Much of the verse was written in rhyming couplets. Today, this form carries little weight in the theatre and is best encountered in pantomimes or Gilbert and Sullivan operettas. In Golden Age France and Spain, the couplet carried the linguistic and emotional weight of the iambic pentameter, and shouldn't be ignored.

Peribanez

Lope De Vega (1605–12), *adapt. Tanya Ronder*

WHO 🖙   *Casilda, wife to Peribanez, a farmer.*

WHERE 🖙   *A wedding party celebration in the marital home in Ocana in the province of Toledo, Spain.*

TO WHOM 🖙   *Her brand new – as of a few minutes – husband. In the company of wedding guests and family including the priest, Casilda's uncle.*

WHEN 🖙   *Contemporary with authorship.*

WHAT HAS JUST HAPPENED 🖙   *Peribanez and Casilda have just got married in the local church and returned home to celebrate. They are not rich, but they are happy. Her husband has just made a speech to honour his new wife, saying he is beyond joy in this marriage, that she is more beautiful to him than anything in his world. This is her response.*

WHAT SHE WANTS/OBJECTIVES TO PLAY 🖙

- *To reciprocate the compliments from her heart.*
- *To make him smile.*
- *To exclaim publicly, openly, honestly, her love and joy in her husband.*

Casilda

❝ Now where do I start? How can I even begin to say everything I feel without my heart breaking open? You make me feel more alive than anything in the world – more than dancing, the music, my pulse, feet racing, drum pounding, the drummer yelling and whooping with all the strength in his throat, my muscles aching from smiling happiness . . . Your voice, the words you choose, lift me more than Midsummer's Day – hearing the cheers come up from the village, smelling lemon verbena and myrtle. What guitar that squeezes my heart could reach me as you do? In your 'how-d'you-do' hat? You mean more to me than my brand new shoes!

You're better than the best banner in the parade, better than the crumbly bread Uncle hands round at Baptisms, better than the Resurrection candle that never goes out. Out of a thousand boys you are the Easter cake covered all over with marzipan chicks and chocolate eggs. No.

She thinks, then she speaks.

You're a young bull in a green field or a clean white shirt folded in a basket of jasmine flowers. You – you're my Pedro. You're you. That's it, I've nothing left to compare you with. **99**

The Misanthrope

Molière (1666), *trans. Stephen Mulrine*

WHO ☞   *Célimène, a young widow (pronounced say-lee-*MEN*).*

WHERE ☞   *Célimène's drawing-room.*

TO WHOM ☞   *Arsinoe (pronounced ar-*SEEN*-oh-eh), her 'friend'.*

WHEN ☞   *Written and set in 1666.*

WHAT HAS JUST HAPPENED ☞   *Célimène is very much a modern woman. She is vivacious, eloquent, entertaining, hugely popular, smart . . . and swamped by would-be suitors, one of whom, the rather austere and 'misanthropic' Alceste, is also the love interest of the pious spinster, Arsinoe. Arsinoe is desperate that Alceste give up on her rival for his affections, and does much to sully Célimène's reputation in his eyes through slanderous and vicious incrimination. She has just arrived, under the guise of offering friendly advice, to make a number of wounding and ill-founded allegations about Célimène's social life and the volume of male acquaintances that swarm her apartment daily. Célimène is advised to watch her behaviour as people are gossiping about her loose morality. Célimène is livid, seeing through the thinly veiled indictments, but maintains a polite façade while she repays Arsinoe in her own style, charging her with hypocrisy and false primness, also in the name of 'friendship'.*

WHAT SHE WANTS/OBJECTIVES TO PLAY ☞

- *To retaliate: this is a response to a disgraceful swipe made by Arsinoe. It is sport, and she, Célimène, is the better player, and is relishing the retaliation.*
- *To let Arsinoe know that she is wise to her game plan.*
- *To rubbish her false pity, and to let her know the truth of her hypocrisy, and that the social construct of devoutness and dutifulness created by her is a sham that everyone sees through.*

- *To unleash all she has secretly felt about her 'devout' friend, but never said.*

TEXT NOTE ☞   *The translation uses rhymed pentameters to mirror the spirit of the original rhyme. The same rules apply for the playing as in the Renaissance iambic pentameter, that is the rhythmic pulse moves the text like a heartbeat, so enjoy that vibration without making it sound like 'verse', it is just how she speaks.*

Célimène

❝ Madame, I'm deeply grateful for such good
Advice – so much so that I feel I should
Return the favour now, without delay,
And offer *you* advice, which, strange to say,
Likewise concerns a reputation – yours.
These people gossip about my *amours*,
And in a show of friendship, you decide
To tell me? I'll let that example guide
Me, then, and as a friend, pass on a word
Or two about yourself – just things I've heard,
Of course. I paid a call the other day
To a certain house, and there, I'm bound to say,
I too found some extremely pious folk
Discussing qualities that all bespoke
A truly moral life. The conversation
Turned to you, Madame, and condemnation
Was widespread of your familiar pose
Of spotless virtue, while your vulgar shows
Of zeal, as good examples, were rejected
Out of hand, along with your affected
Gravity, your never-ending, sleep-
Inducing sermons, and the way you greet
The slightest hint of impropriety,
With cries of horror that society
Should be so wicked. The most innocent
Suggestion can be turned to represent

A smutty *double entendre* in your eyes.
Your high opinion of yourself, likewise,
Was noted, and that vinegary smile
You save for others, full of pity, while
You read them moral lectures on their flaws,
Quite blameless though they be. So it's because
Of these things – and I'm only quoting *them*,
Madame – that these so pious folk condemn
Your way of life. 'What use is it', they said,
'When outward shows of virtue are betrayed
By all the rest? She beats her breast in fervent
Prayer, then calmly turns to beat her servant –
Whom moreover she neglects to pay!
Among the faithful few she makes great play
Of her devotion, yet she paints her face
To hide the ravages of time. She'll place
A portrait of a nude behind a screen,
To spare our blushes, but she's rather keen,
It seems, on flesh and blood reality!'
Well, I spoke up for your morality,
Of course, assured them there was not a grain
Of truth in these vile slanders. All the same,
They clung to their opinion, and concluded
That you were, unhappily, deluded
In attempting to dictate how folk behave;
Far better, they averred, to try and save
Your own soul first, and take a long hard look
At that, before you bring the world to book.
In short, your life should be a shining light,
If you're intending to put others right.
Or better still, if reformation's wanted,
Leave that task to those whom God has granted
The authority. Madame, I trust
You'll take this counsel in good part. You must
Believe me, I too have no axe to grind –
Your interests are all I have in mind. **99**

The Learned Ladies

Molière (1672), *trans. AR Waller,*
adapt. Stephen Pimlott and Colin Chambers

WHO ☞ *Henriette, early 20s, daughter of the wealthy Chrysale and Philaminte.*

WHERE ☞ *In her home.*

TO WHOM ☞ *Trissotin, a poet whom her mother has lined up as a husband for her.*

WHEN ☞ *1659, though this translation releases it from any specific time period.*

WHAT HAS JUST HAPPENED ☞ *Henriette lives within a divided family – divided between head and heart. She is very much like her father, Chrysale, gentle, emotional and straight-forward but ultimately powerless. Her mother, Philaminte, on the other hand is all powerful – a philosopher and leading member of the literati, obsessed with learning, language, thought and poetry and somewhat ashamed of Henriette's lack of literary aspiration. Trissotin has wormed his way into Philaminte's affections, with his phoney and sycophantic appreciation of her work, and she believes he will raise her daughter's reputation and literary standing, through marriage. This is the first opportunity Henriette has had to talk with Trissotin alone since the engagement was proposed. She intends to put him right, to make clear she has no intention of marrying him, not least because she suspects he feels nothing for her but is hoping to marry into her family's wealth. Henriette is actually in love with a very different man, Clitandre, the sort of man her mother loathes and her father loves, and he is very much in love with her; they are like-minded souls, against all things superficial, and both despise what Trissotin stands for – the shallow and dishonest veneer of society life. If only they could persuade her mother.*

WHAT SHE WANTS/OBJECTIVES TO PLAY ☞

- *To warn him that she has seen through the 'philosophical' to the more 'fiscal' interest he has in her.*

- *To keep the communication formal and at arm's length, it is a business-like transaction.*

- *To flatter him by appealing to his vanity and egotism into accepting that her heart lies with a man less worthy than he, but 'c'est la vie' . . .*

- *To teach him through his own subjects – philosophy and poetry – that love is not logical – it is ephemeral and undefinable and so beyond either of them to reason with.*

- *To shame him into releasing the hold he has over her mother, and so over her.*

Henriette

❝ I wish, Monsieur, to speak to you privately about the marriage my mother has in view; I thought that, seeing the trouble into which the house is cast, I might be able to persuade you to listen to reason. I know you believe that my alliance with you will bring you a well-endowed bride; but money, by which so many people set store, is, to a true philosopher, but a worthless allurement; and contempt of riches and of empty display ought not to reveal itself only in your words.

[TRISSOTIN. And it is not in that respect that you charm me; your brilliant beauty, your sweet and penetrating looks, your grace, your bearing, are the dowry, the wealth, which have attracted my desires and tender feelings towards you: they are the sole riches with which I am in love.]

I am very grateful to you for your generous passion: such devoted love overwhelms me and I regret, Monsieur, I am unable to respond to it. I esteem you as much as it is possible to esteem another; but there is an obstacle in the way of my loving you: a heart, you know, cannot belong to two people, and I feel that Clitandre has made himself master of mine.

I am aware that he has much less merit than you, that I show but sorry taste in the choice of a husband, that you possess a hundred fine talents which ought to cause me to prefer you; I see clearly that I am wrong, but I cannot help it; the only effect reason has on me is to make me reproach myself for being so blind.

[TRISSOTIN. The gift of your hand, to which I am permitted to aspire, will set free the heart Clitandre possesses; and I venture to presume that, by means of a thousand little attentions, I shall discover the art of making myself beloved.]

No: my heart is bound by its first inclinations and cannot be touched, Monsieur, by your attentions. I venture to open my heart freely to you in this matter, and my confession contains nothing that ought to offend you. It is common knowledge that the passionate love which sets fire to hearts is not created by merit: caprice is responsible for a share in it, and often, when someone takes our fancy, we cannot tell the reason why. If we could love, Monsieur, to order, and according to the dictates of prudence, you should possess my whole heart and my affection; but we know that love is not thus controlled. Leave me, I pray you, to my blindness and do not profit by that violation of my feelings proposed to be forced upon me. An honourable man does not like to take advantage of the power parents have over us; he shrinks with repugnance from the sacrifice to him of the being he loves, and he is content only with the heart he himself has won. Refrain from urging my mother to exercise her supreme authority over me in her choice; withdraw your offer and bestow upon another the homage of a heart as inestimable as is yours. 〟

Phedra

Racine (1677), *trans. Julie Rose*

WHO ☞   *Phedra, wife of King Theseus of Athens,*
30s plus.

WHERE ☞   *In a room of the Royal Palace, Athens.*

TO WHOM ☞   *Oenone (pronounced Eenonee) her nurse and*
confidante.

WHEN ☞   *Racine took this Greek myth, and adapted it*
for his own time, though the setting is still very much Athens, 7th
century BC.

WHAT HAS JUST HAPPENED ☞   *Phedra has fallen madly*
in love with her step-son, Hippolytus. Believing her husband to
have been slain when warring away from home, she propositioned
him. He rejected her, in no uncertain terms. In the meantime her
husband came back alive and well and, fearing Hippolytus would
tell what she had done, she falsely accused him of trying to assault
her. When confronted by his father Hippolytus denied the charge,
but revealed his love for the captive princess, Aricia. Theseus has
sent Hippolytus away and called on Neptune to punish his son.
Feeling her sins, Phedra wants to clear Hippolytus's name, but
then she hears that he loves Aricia and not her, and is furious.

WHAT SHE WANTS/OBJECTIVES TO PLAY ☞

- *To vent her rage and sexual humiliation.*

- *To get real and practical help to ease her agony and to be*
  prevented from doing anything rash that will further
  compromise her situation.

- *To masochistically torment herself with the news of his love*
  for another and for not even tasting any of the pleasure that
  would have been a consolation for this pain.

- *To speak out loud the outrage that is her life, with no one to*
  turn to, not even her own father.

Phedra

❝   They will always love one another.
Even as I speak, ah! Perish the thought!
They're laughing at this madwoman.
Despite his exile which will separate them,
They swear never to part.
No, I can't bear their happiness – it's poisoning me,
Oenone. Pity me in my jealous rage.
We must get rid of Aricia. We must remind my husband
How he hates her loathsome race.
He must not draw the line at some light sentence:
The sister has outdone her murderous brothers.
I'll implore him in my jealous frenzy.
What am I doing? Am I out of my mind?
Me, jealous! Implore Theseus of all people!
My husband's alive, and my heart's still burning!
And who for? Who do I yearn for?
My every word makes my hair stand on end.
I've sunk as low as I can go.
I am incest and deceit incarnate now.
I want my hands dripping with innocent blood!
Monster! Yet I go on living; can still stare back at
The sacred sun from whom I am descended!
I am descended from the ruler of the Gods;
The heavens, the whole universe is filled with my ancestors.
Where can I hide? I could slip down into hell's dark night.
No I can't! My father's the keeper of the urn of the dead there;
Fate, they say, placed it in his stern hands:
Minos judges the quivering dead in hell.
Ah! Won't his appalled ghost shiver
When his daughter presents herself to him,
Forced to confess so many different sins,
And crimes perhaps unheard of even in hell!
What will you say, father, confronted by that horrible sight?
I believe I see you drop the dreaded urn;
I see you try to dream up some new punishment,
And turn into your own daughter's tormentor.

Forgive me. A cruel goddess has ruined your family;
Can't you see, your sex-crazed daughter's her revenge!
Oh, but my poor body's never even fed
On that forbidden fruit I'm dying of desire for.
Catastrophe has pursued me to the bitter end;
In dying, I give up nothing but pain and turmoil. 〝

Restoration and Eighteenth Century

The Restoration refers to the 'restoration' of the monarchy, the return of Charles II from exile in France, and the end of the Puritan stranglehold on the arts. Theatres that had been closed were reopened, while new ones were built. Indoor theatres grew in popularity, which changed the whole ambience and atmosphere of playgoing, with candlelit evening performances becoming the norm.

The acting became more playful than before, less declamatory, less epic, and gave birth to the domestic 'comedy of manners', investigating, commenting on and criticising a newly licentious world. Wit and wordplay were the most obvious characteristics of the new theatrical language. Themes included the rural idyll of the country against the cynical and superficial town, the corruption of innocence, the social necessity of marrying for property rather than love, and the consequent eruption of adultery.

The Restoration was about sex, and the playing of its delicious language is like sport – a blood sport! Treat the text like a musical score: play it exactly as it is written in terms of its sentence structure, and don't under- or overplay the running motifs or cunning *double entendres.*

Body language was just as important as anything spoken, and a complex system of pointers and signs was established. The lady's fan was not so much a tool for cooling herself as a highly sophisticated communication device. By fanning herself slowly a woman meant 'I am married'; fanning quickly and she was engaged; and twirling the fan in the right hand meant 'I love another'.

Eighteenth-century writing replaced the Restoration's bawdy overtones with a much more genteel sensibility, but the comedy of manners reached another highpoint in Sheridan, from whom there is a direct line through to the comedies of Oscar Wilde and Noël Coward. The language is decidedly more accessible than the Restoration. It almost feels modern, though it still has that period colour, verve and sharpness of wit.

The eighteenth century was a romantic, morally reformative era of society and creativity, bridging the gap between the Restoration and the highground of Victorian manners. Within the drama of this period there was a sneaking sense of the censorious melodrama to come, the beginnings of a complete reversal of Restoration values – or lack of them.

The Country Wife

William Wycherley (1675)

WHO ☞   *Margery, a simple and naive young beauty from the country, new wife of the older Mr Pinchwife. Late teens/20s.*

WHERE ☞   *Margery's bedchamber in their London apartment.*

TO WHOM ☞   *To herself.*

WHEN ☞   *Contemporary with authorship.*

WHAT HAS JUST HAPPENED ☞   *Pinchwife has done everything to stop his young bride from meeting with the notorious womaniser, Horner. He has even made her dress as a boy to meet her need to go out into society, in case he should spot her. But Horner certainly did spot this beautiful newcomer: he saw through the disguise immediately, and found a way to be alone with the 'boy', and promptly propositioned her. Margery has innocently admitted as much to her husband who makes her write a letter to Horner, dictated by him, indicating he should stay away. However, when Pinchwife leaves the room, Margery, in this scene, writes another letter to encourage Horner; she intends to switch it with the first letter. The second part of the speech comes from a later scene, where she shows a burgeoning awareness of her own sexuality and needs, but it works well with this moment.*

WHAT SHE WANTS/OBJECTIVES TO PLAY ☞

- *To persuade herself to do what her husband has ordered her do. To obey his command.*

- *To not offend Mr Horner by doing her husband's bidding.*

- *To express herself like a 'lady of quality' as opposed to the country bumpkin she is.*

- *To encourage Horner in his desires, and to become a woman of the world.*

- *To enjoy the sensation of flirting, albeit in writing – this is a new game to her and a far cry from her relationship with Pinchwife.*

Margery

❝ 'For Mr Horner' – so, I am glad he has told me his name. Dear Mr Horner – but why should I send thee such a letter, that will vex thee, and make thee angry with me? Well, I will not send it – Ay, but then my husband will kill me – for I see plainly, he won't let me love Mr Horner. But what care I for my husband? I won't, so I won't, send poor Mr Horner such a letter – but then my husband – But oh, what if I writ at bottom my husband made me write it? Ay, but then my husband would see't. Can one have no shift? Ah, a London woman would have had a hundred presently. Stay – what if I should write a letter, and wrap it up like this, and write upon't too? Ay, but then my husband would see't. I don't know what to do – but yet y'vads I'll try, so I will – for I will not send this letter to poor Mr Horner, come what will on't.

She writes and repeats what she hath writ.

'Dear, sweet Mr Horner,' – so – 'My husband would have me send you a base, rude, unmannerly letter, but I won't' – so – 'and would have me forbid you loving me, but I won't' – so – 'and would have me say to you, I hate you, poor Mr Horner, but I won't tell a lie for him' – there – 'for I'm sure if you and I were in the country at cards together' – so – 'I could not help treading on your toe under the table' – so – 'or rubbing knees with you, and staring in your face, till you saw me' – very well – 'and then looking down, and blushing for an hour together,' – so – 'but I must make haste before my husband comes; and now he has taught me to write letters, you shall have longer ones from me, who am,

Dear, dear, poor, dear Mr Horner,

Your most humble friend, and servant to command till death, Margery Pinchwife.'

Well, 'tis e'en so; I have got the London disease they call love. I am sick of my husband, and for my gallant. I have heard this distemper called a fever but methinks 'tis liker an ague, for when I think of my husband I tremble and am in a cold sweat and have inclinations to vomit: but when I think of my gallant, dear Mr Horner, my hot fit comes and I am all in a fever, indeed, and as in other fevers my own chamber is tedious to me, and I would fain be removed to his, and then methinks I should be well. Ah, poor Mr Horner! **99**

GLOSSARY

Can one have no shift? Is there no strategem available?
y'vads in faith

She Ventures, and He Wins

Ariadne (1695)

WHO ☞   *Charlotte, a rich heiress, early 20s.*

WHERE ☞   *A London street.*

TO WHOM ☞   *Her cousin Juliana.*

WHEN ☞   *Contemporary with authorship.*

WHAT HAS JUST HAPPENED ☞   *Charlotte's plot is to win a husband who desires her for herself rather than for her fortune. In this opening scene both she and her cousin Juliana are dressed in men's clothing. She explains why they are dressed as such while at the same time offering Juliana a masterclass in gender politics!*

WHAT SHE WANTS/OBJECTIVES TO PLAY ☞

- *To educate her more naïve cousin in the ways of this shallow world they inhabit.*

- *To convince Juliana that somewhere out there is a man worthy of her love: she just needs to find him.*

- *To recruit a fellow smart woman who won't pander to men offering themselves as prospective husbands – whether they be hard-working bores looking for someone to keep house, or vain dandies hoping to seize upon a woman's fortune.*

- *To mock the tactics and vanities of men who attempt to woo her with false flattery.*

Charlotte

❝ Why, to ramble the town till I can meet with the man I can find in my heart to take for better for worse. These clothes will give us greater liberty then the scandalous world will allow to our petticoats, which we could not attempt this undertaking in without hazard to our modesty. Besides, should I meet with the man whose outside pleased me, 'twill be impossible by any other means to discover his humour; for they are so used to flatter and deceive our sex, that there's nothing but the angel appears, though the devil lies lurking within, and never so much as shows his paw till he has got his prey fast in his clutches. [. . .]

No, my dear Julia, to avoid it is the scope of my design; for, though by laziness and ease the generality of mankind is degenerated into a soft effeminacy, unworthy of the noble stamp was set upon their soul; there still remains a race retains the image Heaven made them in, virtuous, and just, sincere and brave: and such a one I'll find, if I search to the Antipodes for him, or else lead apes in Hell. [. . .]

No sure: none can think one of my youth and fortune can want the tenders of hearts enough; I'm not obliged to follow the world's dull maxims, nor will I wait for the formal address of some ceremonious coxcomb, with more land than brains, who would bargain for us as he would for his horse, and talks of nothing but taxes and hard times, to make me a good housewife; or else some gay young fluttering thing, who calls himself a Beau, and wants my fortune to maintain him in that character: such an opinionated animal, who believes there needs no more to reach a lady's heart than a *bon mien*, fine dress, the periwig well adjusted, the hand well managed in taking snuff, to show the fine diamond ring, if he's worth one; sometimes a conceited laugh, with the mouth stretched from one ear to t'other, to discover the white teeth, with sneak and cringe in an affected tone cries, 'Damn me, Madam, if you are not the prettiest creature my eyes ere saw! 'Tis impossible for me to live if you are so cruel to deny me,' with a world of such foolish stuff, which they talk all by rote. No, my Julia, I'll have one who loves my person as well as gold, and please myself, not the world, in my choice. **99**

GLOSSARY

lead apes in Hell the proverbial fate of spinsters
coxcomb fool
bon mien polite bearing, good manners
by rote by heart, parrot-fashion

The Royal Mischief

Delariviere Manley (1696)

WHO ☞ *Bassima, daughter of the ruler of Abca, recently conquered in war. 20s.*

WHERE ☞ *A room in the Castle of Phasia, in the kingdom of Libardian.*

TO WHOM ☞ *Osman, Chief Visier to the Prince of Libardian.*

WHEN ☞ *A mythical, previous time.*

WHAT HAS JUST HAPPENED ☞ *Bassima was captured by Osman. He fell hopelessly in love with her, though married to the Prince of Libardian's sister. And he has declared his love. Bassima has been married off to the Prince of Colchis, close ally to the Libardians, for political reasons. There is evidently no love between these two. In this scene we witness Bassima finally admitting to her feelings for Osman, a terrible love for him; it will surely lead to the collapse of her virtue and the destruction of her life: she will not be able to resist his advances, as she has been able to do since her capture, and so she implores him to desist.*

WHAT SHE WANTS/OBJECTIVES TO PLAY ☞

- *To look for some explanation from on high about this terrible predicament.*

- *To admit the full and awesome extent of her love, to explain its dire consequences if pursued and to let him go – for both their sakes.*

- *To make him see his actions and declarations are inappropriate and fanciful – and that to continue thus would lead to the destruction of them both.*

- *To beg him to take responsibility, to take her fate in his hands, to protect her from her own desires by choosing to go away or to ignore her.*

- *To remind him they cannot do what God forbids: she has lived with that possibility, and has been terrified by it.*

Bassima

"   O thou
Eternal power that first made fate,
If I have sinn'd, 'twas by your own decree.
Why send you passion of desire and joy
And then command us those passions to destroy,
When long forseeing that we can't do so,
Dooms us rewards of everlasting woe?
Where's then the kindness to their likeness shown,
Cast in a form they vainly call their own?
Fond ignorance, for they are all divine,
Exempt from what unhappy mortals fear,
Nor can their beings fail, like those who wander here.
Hence, then, thou false receiv'd belief, be gone,
And let us see we're like ourselves alone.

[OSMAN. Who gives my princess grief?]

                                    You, only you.
The Earth's united hatred could not harm
Me equal to your kindness. It strikes at
Innocence and fame, and lays my virtue
Level with the vilest,
Makes marriage an uneasy bondage,
And the embraces of my lord a loathsome
Penance. What would you more? The time is come
That I must speak to make my ruin certain.
Like some prophetic priestess, full of the
God that rends her, must breathe the baleful
Oracle or burst. My crowding stars just
Now appear to fight, and dart upon me
With malignant influence. Nor can my
Reason stop the dictates of my heart,
They echo from my mouth in sounds of love,
But such a love as never woman knew.

'Twas surely given by fate, I would have said
From Heaven, but that inspires but good,
And this is surely none.

[OSMAN. The good is all to come. The ill is past.
Believe me, Madam, I who feel the change
The happy turn, your kind complaint, has brought
Though I, before thought life a worthless rag
A garment of too vile a price to wear
Would not now change it for a monarch's state.]

You draw too nigh,
For fenc'd about with chastity and glory,
Which like a magic circle shall enfold me,
You must not hope to pass the sacred round,
Lest sure destruction prove our lot forever. [. . .]

You like a lover entertain your fancy,
But I have still the fatal land in view,
Where death of honour waits on that of life.
Now let us part, lest we should meet on that. [. . .]

My inauspicious fate comes fast upon me.
You, only you, can stop its headlong course.
I charge you then, by honour, glory, fame,
By love, the mighty god that now torments me,
You yield me not, a sinful slave, to death,
Torn in my conscience, mangled in my virtue,
But fly from hence, never to see me more.
Or should you stay, dare not to meet my eyes
With yours, those tell-tales of your passion,
Lest I break rudely from my husband's arms,
And fly to death in yours. 〃

The Fatal Friendship

Catherine Trotter (1698)

WHO ☞   *Lamira, a beautiful and wealthy widow. 20s.*

WHERE ☞   *In Lamira's bedroom.*

TO WHOM ☞   *Gramont, her husband of a few hours.*

WHEN ☞   *In France after 'a war against Spain', so*
referring back to a slightly earlier time than authorship.

WHAT HAS JUST HAPPENED ☞   *Lamira has loved Gramont*
for a long time, above all others. She has had no indication from
him that he reciprocates this love, but he has suddenly had a change
of heart, insisting on a quick marriage – a few hours previous to
this scene. But it has had to be in secret as her deceased husband's
will stated her fortune was to pass to his sister should she re-
marry. However, Gramont does not love her; in fact he secretly
married his childhood sweetheart Felicia two years previously.
They have a son, cared for from afar. But recently pirates have
captured that son; Gramont knows the only route to his release
lies in a ransom, and a huge one. So this marriage is bigamous,
but Lamira is rich and he will have access to her money, and
Felicia and the world at large need never know about it. But he
has no intention of consummating the marriage, as Lamira is
about to discover during this first midnight of their marriage.

WHAT SHE WANTS/OBJECTIVES TO PLAY ☞

- *To secure his loving response to her declaration of love: to*
  tease him with gentle reproach.

- *To terrify him with her totally rational condemnation: to let*
  him know the fearful price to be paid should he ever dare see
  this other woman again; and to advise him, in an entirely
  reasonable way, that his life will never be the same again:
  that he – and this woman, are about to go to hell.

- *To make him aware that she is his superior both morally and*
  intellectually and that he will pay the price of that inequality.

- *To belittle him, diminish him and patronise him.*

Lamira

" I have no thought, no wish beyond your love;
Make me secure of that, and I am blest.
Why are thou thus unmov'd, thou cruel savage?
Hast thou no sensibility, no fire in thy soul?
Or have not I the art to blow the flame?
Instruct me then, if 'tis not yet too late,
If 'tis not kindled at another's charms.
That was an injurious thought, chide it away,
Tell me you could not be so false, so base.
You do not answer!
Nay, then I fear I am abus'd indeed.
Speak quickly, swear I am not, the very fear's
Distracting, not to be borne, swear you are thus by nature,
Thus cold, insensible to all the sex
As you are now to me, swear that,
And I'll complain no more of your indifference,
But with submissive duty, tenderest care,
And most unwearied love, still strive to move
Thy cold, obdurate heart. Is there a hope to gain it?

[GRAMONT. Madam you set it at too high a rate,
It is not worth your least concern or thought.]

Why, why inhuman dost thou answer thus
Regardless of the doubts that rack my soul
Oh speak, reply to them, e'er they distract me
'Tis enough enough. Thy silence speaks
The dumb confession of a guilty mind.
Ay, there it is, thou false, perfidious man!
'Tis to a rival I am sacrific'd.
But think'st thou I will tamely bear my wrongs,
And let her triumph in 'em? Dare not to see her,
For, if thou dost, I'll find the strumpet out.
Confusion! Slighted, for another, too!
Oh, how I'll be reveng'd! I'll know this sorceress,
Make her most infamous,
I'll be your plague, anticipate your hell! [. . .]

Dissembling,
Vilest wretch! Thou thing below my anger!
There have been glorious villains that may look
With scorn on thee, disdaining thy low ends;
A paltry bait of fortune, poor spirited,
Mean traitor, what indigent abandon'd creature
Is this, that hopes to vaunt it in my spoils,
Yet must be purchas'd at no less a rate
Than such an insolent disdain of me?
What are your terms? What she? And what her charms?
Let's know the state and reason of this preference –
Stubborn and dumb! Am I not worth an answer?

[GRAMONT. Why Madam, can I answer to your rage?]

My wrongs, thy own upbraiding guilt thou can'st not answer.
I do not rage, nor is there any rage
For injuries like this.
All that has had the name of passion, fury,
Even to madness, here is higher reason.
So basely us'd! A rival's property!
Unvalued, thus despis'd for her, tormenting!
What easy fool did'st think thou hast secured?
Mistaken man! Thou hast rous'd a woman's rage,
In spite of all thy harden'd villainy,
Thou shalt repent thou didst provoke me thus.
I'll haunt your steps, and interrupt your joys,
Fright you with curses from your minion's arms,
Pursue you with reproaches, blast her fame.
I'll be the constant bane of all your pleasures,
A jarring, clamorous, very wife to thee,
To her a greater plague than thou to me. **99**

GLOSSARY

perfidious treacherous
minion darling

The Tragedy of Jane Shore

Nicholas Rowe (1714)

WHO ☞　　　*Jane Shore. Mistress of the recently deceased Edward IV. 20s plus.*

WHERE ☞　　　*A street, at the door of her friend Alicia.*

TO WHOM ☞　　*The audience.*

WHEN ☞　　　*1480s.*

WHAT HAS JUST HAPPENED ☞　*It is a politically dangerous time. Edward IV has died, leaving his young son Edward, to take the throne. However, the Duke of Gloucester (the future Richard III) plans to take the throne and has Edward's children placed in the Tower of London. His only obstacle is Lord Hastings, former chamberlain to Edward IV. Gloucester needs evidence of Hastings's rivalry to 'remove' him from the scene, and it comes in an anonymous betrayal by Alicia, Hastings's lover and Jane's friend. Alicia mistakenly believed Jane and Hastings to have rekindled their previous relationship and so, believing herself betrayed, vengefully also implicated Jane as the power behind the plan. Gloucester demands that Hastings is executed; Jane's punishment is to wander the streets as a beggar – she has not eaten in three days and is close to death. Jane has gone from famously honourable lady in mourning for her King and her love, to vagrant, in one fell swoop. Jane speaks this soliloquy as she arrives at Alicia's door, in a desperate state, to plead for charity from, as she believes, her true friend. On the first speech break, a servant opens the door and turns her away. Jane does not know that Alicia has betrayed her.*

WHAT SHE WANTS/OBJECTIVES TO PLAY ☞

- *To be at peace, which means, in her state, to die, that this pain of existence might stop.*

- *To not even try to understand any more but just accept the minutes, maybe hours, until her death.*

- *To receive some comfort before she goes from a dear friend.*
- *To cheer herself with a remembrance of how she used to be received.*

Jane

❝ Yet, yet endure, nor murmur, Oh! My soul!
For are not thy transgressions great and numberless?
Do they not cover thee like rising floods?
And press thee like a weight of waters down?
Does not the hand of righteousness afflict thee?
And who shall plead against it? Who shall say
To Power Almighty: Thou hast done enough?
Or bid His dreadful rod of vengeance stay?
Wait then with patience, till the circling hours
Shall bring the time of thy appointed rest,
And lay thee down in death. The hireling thus
With labour drudges out the painful day,
And often looks with long-expecting eyes
To see the shadows rise and be dismissed.
And hark! Methinks the roar that late pursued me,
Sinks, like the murmurs of a falling wind,
And softens into silence. Does revenge
And malice then grow weary and forsake me?
My guard too, that observed me still so close,
Tire in the task of their inhuman office,
And loiter far behind. [. . .]

[JANE SHORE (*to servant at door*). Tell my Alicia
'Tis I would see her.
SERVANT.   She is ill at ease
And will admit no visitor.
JANE SHORE   But tell her
'Tis I, her friend, the partner of her heart
Wait at the door and beg –
SERVANT.   'Tis all in vain
Go hence, and howl to those that will regard you.
    The door is shut.]

It was not always thus; the time has been
When this unfriendly door that bars my passage
Flew wide, and almost leap'd from off its hinges
To give me entrance here; when this good house
Has pour'd forth all its dwellers to receive me;
When my approach has made a little holy-day,
And ev'ry face was dressed in smiles to meet me.
But now 'tis otherwise, and those who bless'd me
Now curse me to my face. Why should I wander,
Stray further on, for I can die ev'n here! [. . .]

Sure, I am near upon my journey's end;
My head runs round, my eyes begin to fail,
And dancing shadows swim before my sight.
I can no more. (*Lies down.*) Receive me, thou cold earth;
Thou common parent, take me to thy bosom,
And let me rest with thee. **99**

GLOSSARY

hireling day labourer

The London Merchant

George Lillo (1731)

WHO ☞ *Millwood, 'a lady of pleasure' according to the author's cast-list description; a young woman of independent means who has plenty of leisure time. 20s plus.*

WHERE ☞ *Millwood's home.*

TO WHOM ☞ *The officers, her friend Lucy, Trueman and Thorowgood.*

WHEN ☞ *1588.*

WHAT HAS JUST HAPPENED ☞ *Sick of men using women, Millwood has come up with a plan to use a man before he can use her. She has begun charming George Barnwell, the London Merchant apprenticed to Thorowgood. Knowing he is infatuated by her, she instructs him to steal money from his master for her. He obeys but confesses what he has been doing to his fellow apprentice Trueman, who disapproves but is sworn to secrecy. Barnwell again submits to her demands when stealing a bag of money for her from his employer. As a final test to prove his love, Millwood suggests Barnwell kill his beloved uncle and seize his fortune for her. Barnwell is horrified but agrees. He is then overcome by his sin and cannot go ahead with it, so she has him arrested on a trumped-up charge. However, Barnwell does not betray her; instead it is Lucy, Millwood's confidante, whose confession of Millwood's plans to Thorowgood and Trueman leads to Millwood's arrest. This is her response to the arrest.*

WHAT SHE WANTS/OBJECTIVES TO PLAY ☞

- *To educate them in the hypocrisy of their times, and the hypocrisy of piety.*

- *To impress upon them that she has only behaved as is normal in this man's world.*

- *To let them know her greater cause – that of heading the movement of vengeance by women against all men and their intent on women's destruction.*

Millwood

❝ I have done nothing that I am sorry for. I followed my inclinations, and that the best of you does every day. All actions are alike natural and indifferent to man and beast who devour or are devoured as they meet with others weaker or stronger than themselves.

[THOROWGOOD. What pity it is, a mind so comprehensive, daring, and inquisitive should be a stranger to religion's sweet but powerful charms.]

I am not fool enough to be an atheist, though I have known enough of men's hypocrisy to make a thousand simple women so. Whatever religion is in itself, as practised by mankind it has caused the evils you say it was designed to cure. War, plague, and famine has not destroyed so many of the human race as this pretended piety has done, and with such barbarous cruelty as if the only way to honour Heaven were to turn the present world into Hell. [. . .]

What are your laws, of which you make your boast, but the fool's wisdom and the coward's valour, the instrument and screen of all your villainies by which you punish in others what you act yourselves or would have acted, had you been in their circumstances? The judge who condemns the poor man for being a thief had been a thief himself, had he been poor. Thus, you go on deceiving and being deceived, harassing, plaguing, and destroying one another, but women are your universal prey.

Women, by whom you are, the source of joy,
With cruel arts you labour to destroy.
A thousand ways our ruin you pursue,
Yet blame in us those arts first taught by you.
Oh, may, from hence, each violated maid,
By flatt'ring, faithless, barb'rous man betray'd,
When robb'd of innocence and virgin fame,
From your destruction raise a nobler name:
To right their sex's wrongs devote their mind
And future Millwoods prove, to plague mankind! **❞**

The Clandestine Marriage
David Garrick and George Colman the Elder (1766)

WHO ☞   *Miss Stirling, the future Lady Melvil, 20s.*

WHERE ☞   *A chamber in her father's house.*

TO WHOM ☞   *Fanny Stirling, her sister.*

WHEN ☞   *Contemporary with authorship.*

WHAT HAS JUST HAPPENED ☞   *Fanny is secretly engaged to her true love, Lovewell. Her sister suspects the match, but Fanny has always denied the affair. Lovewell is not rich enough to be considered a decent match, and she is protecting him until such time as they can reveal the truth. Miss Sterling prefers riches to love. Fanny insists that she cannot be envious of her sister's forthcoming marriage to Sir John Melvil, a marriage without love, irrespective of the diamonds and gold that may accompany it. Miss Stirling simply does not believe her.*

WHAT SHE WANTS/OBJECTIVES TO PLAY ☞

- *To get her sister to admit that she, Miss Stirling, has by far the better prospects in marrying for money.*

- *To belittle and diminish her sister's non-materialistic aspirations.*

- *To dazzle her with an illustration of what her married life will be.*

- *To make her sister jealous. To 'mortify' her.*

- *To thoroughly indulge her fantasies of life to come – Miss Stirling is speaking her projected image out loud as much for herself as anyone else, her appetite for that life is insatiable and palpable in every vivid description/re-enactment.*

Miss Stirling

❝ Oh, my dear sister, say no more! This is downright hypocrisy. You shall never convince me that you don't envy me beyond measure. Well, after all it is extremely natural. It is impossible to be angry with you. [. . .] But I had forgot. There's that dear sweet creature Mr Lovewell in the case. You would not break your faith with your true love now for the world, I warrant you. [. . .] Pretty peevish soul! Oh, my dear, grave, romantic sister! – A perfect philosopher in petticoats! Love and a cottage! Eh, Fanny! Ah, give me indifference and a coach and six! [. . .] (*Aside.*) I must mortify her a little. – I know you have a pretty taste. Pray, give me your opinion of my jewels. How d'ye like the style of this esclavage? (*Showing jewels.*) [. . .] What d'ye think of these bracelets? I shall have a miniature of my father, set round with diamonds, to one, and Sir John's to the other. And this pair of ear-rings! Set transparent! Here, the tops, you see, will take off to wear in a morning, or in an undress. How d'ye like them? [. . .] I have a bouquet to come home tomorrow – made up of diamonds, and rubies, and emeralds, and topazes, and amethysts – jewels of all colours, green, red, blue, yellow, intermixed – the prettiest thing you ever saw in your life! The jeweller says I shall set out with as many diamonds as anybody in town, except Lady Brilliant, and Polly What-d'ye-call-it, Lord Squander's kept mistress. [. . .] Oh, how I long to be transported to the dear regions of Grosvenor Square – far – far from the dull districts of Aldersgate, Cheap, Candlewick, and Farringdon Without and Within! My heart goes pit-a-pat at the very idea of being introduced at Court! – gilt chariot! – piebald horses ! – laced liveries! – and then the whispers buzzing round the circle: 'Who is that young lady? Who is she?' 'Lady Melvil, ma'am!' Lady Melvil! My ears tingle at the sound. And then at dinner, instead of my father perpetually asking: 'Any news upon 'Change?' to cry: 'Well, Sir John! Anything new from Arthur's?' – or to say to some other woman of quality: 'Was your ladyship at the Duchess of Rubber's last night? – Did you call in at Lady Thunder's? In the immensity of crowd I swear I did not see you – Scarce a soul at the opera last Saturday. – Shall I see you at Carlisle House next Thursday?' – Oh, the dear beau-monde! I was born to move in the sphere of the great world. ❞

GLOSSARY

esclavage necklace
beau-monde high society

The Rivals

Richard Brinsley Sheridan (1775)

WHO ☞ *Lydia Languish, a beautiful, headstrong and romantic young heiress. Early 20s.*

WHERE ☞ *In her cousin Julia's dressing room.*

TO WHOM ☞ *Julia.*

WHEN ☞ *Contemporary with authorship.*

WHAT HAS JUST HAPPENED ☞ *Lydia wants to marry for love, not money, and plans to elope with penniless Ensign Beverley. She knows well that if she does, her formidable aunt, Mrs Malaprop, will disinherit her. This all rather adds to the glamour of the situation for her. Beverley is actually an alias for Captain Jack Absolute. He loves Lydia and knows her well enough to understand he will be better off pursuing her as a mere Ensign, knowing her passion for a dangerous liaison with all the thrill of subversion. But when Jack's father, Sir Anthony Absolute, suggests to Mrs Malaprop that Jack and Lydia should marry, Lydia discovers his true identity and rejects him. She is heartbroken – she never imagined she would be involved in such a conventional romance. She has a deep loathing for conformity and cannot possibly associate it either with true love or with him.*

WHAT SHE WANTS/OBJECTIVES TO PLAY ☞

- *To vent her rage, her bitter disappointment and her deeply-felt betrayal.*

- *To let her cousin know that she will never accept the man she loves in this, his real, persona.*

- *To reinforce her sense of her true self – a woman defined by totally romantic sensibilities.*

- *To be consoled and comforted.*

- *To pour scorn and contempt on conventional marriages.*

Lydia Languish

❝ Why, is it not provoking, when I thought we were coming to the prettiest distress imaginable, to find myself made a mere Smithfield bargain of at last? – There had I projected one of the most sentimental elopements! – so becoming a disguise! – so amiable a ladder of ropes! Conscious moon – four horses – Scotch parson – with such surprise to Mrs Malaprop – and such paragraphs in the newspapers! – Oh, I shall die with disappointment.

[JULIA. I don't wonder at it!]

Now – sad reverse!- what have I to expect, but, after a deal of flimsy preparation with a bishop's licence, and my aunt's blessing, to go simpering up to the altar; or perhaps be cried three times in a country church, and have an unmannerly fat clerk ask the consent of every butcher in the parish to join John Absolute and Lydia Languish, spinster! Oh, that I should live to hear myself called spinster!

[JULIA. Melancholy, indeed!]

How mortifying, to remember the dear delicious shifts I used to be put to, to gain half a minute's conversation with this fellow! How often have I stole forth, in the coldest night in January, and found him in the garden, stuck like a dripping statue! There would he kneel to me in the snow, and sneeze and cough so pathetically! He shivering with cold, and I with apprehension! And while the freezing blast numbed our joints, how warmly would he press me to pity his flame, and glow with mutual ardour! – Ah, Julia! That was something like being in love. ❞

GLOSSARY

Smithfield bargain object of a cattle auction
cried three times i.e. the announcement of marriage banns
shifts tricks

The Rivals

Richard Brinsley Sheridan (1775)

WHO ☞   *Julia, a sensible and extremely intelligent
young woman, 20s.*

WHERE ☞   *In Julia's dressing room.*

TO WHOM ☞   *Faulkland, her fiancé.*

WHEN ☞   *Contemporary with authorship.*

WHAT HAS JUST HAPPENED ☞   *Her parents now both dead,
Julia has been engaged for a year to an old family friend and
dearest love, Faulkland. However he is a man so obsessively
jealous that even she is driven to distraction at times by his
bizarre behaviour. In this scene he has again tested her, saying
some dreadful incident has occurred and he needs to leave the
country straight away. She is distraught, insists on going with
him and agrees to honour their engagement by marrying straight
away. Then it transpires there was no incident: he wanted to see
her reaction. Julia has had enough.*

WHAT SHE WANTS/OBJECTIVES TO PLAY ☞

- *To let go of him, for the sake of her own sanity – the
  engagement has run out of time for her. A year on and he is
  still prevaricating and tormenting her.*

- *To go as far as she can to change, once and for all, his behaviour.
  To shock him out of the character he has chosen to be.*

- *To make him feel as terrible as she was just now made to feel:
  to give him a taste of his own medicine.*

- *To teach him the most important lesson – he needs to address
  his behaviour and change for himself; she is no longer even in
  the picture. He has to know now what he has lost to make this
  change.*

- *To remind Faulkland of her bereavement; and how he has
  betrayed her father's memory, in treating her, someone so
  vulnerable, so poorly.*

Julia

66 Hold, Faulkland! – that you are free from a crime, which I before feared to name, Heaven knows how sincerely I rejoice! These are tears of thankfulness for that! But that your cruel doubts should have urged you to an imposition that has wrung my heart, gives me now a pang more keen than I can express.

[FAUKLAND. By Heavens! Julia –]

Yet hear me. – My father loved you, Faulkland! And you preserved the life that tender parent gave me; in his presence I pledged my hand – joyfully pledged it – where before I had given my heart. When, soon after, I lost that parent, it seemed to me that providence had, in Faulkland, shown me whither to transfer, without a pause, my grateful duty, as well as my affection. Hence I have been content to bear from you what pride and delicacy would have forbid from another. I will not upbraid you, by repeating how you have trifled with my sincerity –

[FAULKAND. I confess it all! Yet hear –]

After such a year of trial – I might have flattered myself that I should not have been insulted with a new probation of my sincerity, as cruel as unnecessary! I now see it is not in your nature to be content, or confident in love. With this conviction – I never will be yours. While I had hopes that my persevering attention, and unreproaching kindness might in time reform your temper, I should have been happy to have gained a dearer influence over you; but I will not furnish you with a licensed power to keep alive an incorrigible fault, at the expense of one who never would contend with you.

[FAULKLAND. Nay, but Julia, by my soul and honour, if after this –]

But one word more. As my faith has once been given to you, I never will barter it with another. I shall pray for your happiness, with the truest sincerity; and the dearest blessing I can ask of Heaven to send you, will be to charm you from that unhappy temper, which alone has prevented the performance of our solemn engagement. All I request of you is, that you will yourself reflect upon this infirmity, and when you number up the many true delights it has deprived you of – let it not be your least regret, that it lost you the love of one who would have followed you in beggary through the world! **99**

GLOSSARY

probation proof

The Critic

Richard Brinsley Sheridan (1779)

WHO ☞   *Mrs Dangle, the wife of a theatre critic,*
30s plus.

WHERE ☞   *At the breakfast table.*

TO WHOM ☞   *Her husband, the critic, Mr Dangle.*

WHEN ☞   *Contemporary with authorship.*

WHAT HAS JUST HAPPENED ☞   *The play follows a day in the life of would-be professional impresario and critic Mr Dangle, and this speech comes from the opening scene of the play, setting up many of its themes. Mrs Dangle reads the paper for hard news and politics, and is convinced an invasion by foreigners is imminent. Mr Dangle, however, is obsessed only by affairs of the theatre. To his wife's dismay, now the season has started, their home has become a centre for fellow-critics, actors and playwrights. Here, Mr Dangle is about to regale his wife with details of a new play by author, Mr Puff, when she responds as follows.*

WHAT SHE WANTS/OBJECTIVES TO PLAY ☞

- *To ridicule him out of this obsessive 'hobby'.*

- *To remind him of the real affairs of the day – the politics.*

- *To diminish and rubbish the whims and fashions of the theatre and those who ply that trade.*

- *To stop him speaking on the subject – ever again!*

Mrs Dangle

❝ Lord, Mr Dangle, why will you plague me about such nonsense? – Now the plays are begun I shall have no peace. – Isn't it sufficient to make yourself ridiculous by your passion for the theatre, without continually teasing me to join you?

Why can't you ride your hobby horse without desiring to place me on a pillion behind you, Mr Dangle?

[DANGLE. Nay, my dear, I was only going to read –]

No, no; you never will read anything that's worth listening to: you hate to hear about your country; there are letters every day with Roman signatures, demonstrating the certainty of an invasion, and proving that the nation is utterly undone – but you never will read anything to entertain one.

[DANGLE. What has a woman to do with politics, Mrs Dangle?]

And what have you to do with the theatre, Mr Dangle? Why should you affect the character of a critic? I have no patience with you! – Haven't you made yourself the jest of all your acquaintance by your interference in matters where you have no business? Are you not called a theatrical Quidnunc, and a mock Maecenas to second-hand authors? [. . .]

And to be sure, it is extremely pleasant to have one's house made the motley rendezvous of all the lackeys of literature! – The very high change of trading authors and jobbing critics! – Yes, my drawing room is an absolute register-office for candidate actors, and poets without character; then to be continually alarmed with Misses and Ma'ams piping hysteric changes on Juliets and Dorindas, Pollys and Ophelias; and the very furniture trembling at the probationary starts and unprovoked rants of would-be Richards and Hamlets! – And what is worse than all, now that the manager has monopolised the opera-house, haven't we the signors and signoras calling here, sliding their smooth semibreves, and gargling glib divisions in their outlandish throats – with foreign emissaries and French spies, for ought I know, disguised like fiddlers and figure dancers.

[DANGLE. Mercy! Mrs Dangle!]

And to employ yourself so idly at such an alarming crisis as this too – when, if you had the least spirit, you would have been at the head of one of the Westminster associations – or

trailing a volunteer pike in the Artillery Ground! But you –
o' my conscience, I believe, if the French were landed
tomorrow, you first inquiry would be, whether they had
brought a theatrical troop with them. **99**

GLOSSARY

with Roman signatures signed pseudonymously with the names of
    Roman writers or politicians
Quidnunc busybody
Maecenas patron of the arts
Juliets . . . Dorindas . . . Pollys . . . Ophelias the heroines of *Romeo and
    Juliet*, *The Beaux' Stratagem*, *The Beggar's Opera* and *Hamlet*
signors and signoras opera singers
semibreves sustained notes

Nineteenth and Early Twentieth Centuries

Over the nineteenth and early twentieth centuries, theatre genres included spectacle and melodrama, politically conscious drama, acute social comedy and naturalism.

Melodrama is immediately identifiable as drama that deals primarily with morality. Characters are either good or bad, the issues either black or white; the stakes are always high, and musical accompaniment was the greatest character of all. Many films and much of television soap opera today abide by the principles of melodrama.

By contrast, in the works of Ibsen, Strindberg and Chekhov, nothing happens, seemingly – and yet everything happens. Their plays, written in the last quarter of the nineteenth century and the first years of the twentieth, are domestic in setting, but their themes are huge and primeval: love, loss, freedom (personal as well as national and civic), and death (of an era, or a place, as well as of a human being). The characters talk conversationally, apparently not saying much of significance, but everything is communicated between the words, in the pauses; the subtext is seething with often-unvoiced intentions.

There is an effusive, passionate and poetic element to this writing. The translations selected here reflect the everyday reality of the language, without losing the flavour and weight of the original. It is important not to listen to the latent poetic qualities, or be seduced by the lyricism. Play the text as accurately and in as truthful a way as possible. Stanislavski's system of acting was created to give actors a new way to approach precisely this sort of writing. In preparing these naturalistic speeches, attentive emotional investigation should help you excavate the rich subtext.

Oscar Wilde's work at the very end of the nineteenth century is different. His style developed the witticisms and verbal pyrotechnics of the eighteenth century – writing which looked underneath the polite veneer of society and revealed its shallowness. The sentences are long, the rhythms crucial, and to maximise the comic effect you should only take a breath on a full stop.

George Bernard Shaw takes a step further towards the politicisation of drama. Shaw was a socialist, a fantastically intellectual and liberal thinker, a modernist and a man preoccupied first and foremost with the hypocrisy of the contemporary world. His work heralded socially-conscious drama in Britain, and formed the perfect counterpoint to the trend of naturalism being pioneered in Russia and Scandinavia. His writing needs to be played as a musical score – if you change the puntuation, it will not be 'Shaw'.

Fashion, or Life in New York

Anna Cora Mowatt (1845)

WHO ☞ *Mrs Tiffany, a lady who, according to the author, 'imagines herself fashionable'. Early 30s plus.*

WHERE ☞ *A splendid drawing room in Mrs Tiffany's house, New York.*

TO WHOM ☞ *Millinette, her French maid.*

WHEN ☞ *Contemporary with authorship.*

WHAT HAS JUST HAPPENED ☞ *This speech comes from the opening scene of the play. Mrs Tiffany is a social climber who effects a façade of sophistication and old money, determined to be amongst the New York elite, though she actually has rather more lowly beginnings as a milliner. She is awaiting her guests who include a Count, to whom she hopes to introduce her daughter, Seraphina. Millinette, her maid, specifically brought from Paris, is her invaluable access to the European way of doing things.*

WHAT SHE WANTS/OBJECTIVES TO PLAY ☞

- *To assert her authority and also to win Millinette's approval.*

- *To learn as much as possible from Millinette whilst there is no one around to observe her being taught by a servant!*

- *To create a hierarchy between the new servant, her maid and herself.*

Mrs Tiffany

❝ Is everything in order, Millinette? Ah! Very elegant, very elegant, indeed! There is a jenny-says-quoi look about this furniture – an air of fashion and gentility perfectly bewitching. Is there not, Millinette? [. . .] But where is Miss Seraphina? It is twelve o'clock; our visitors will be pouring in, and she has not made her appearance. But I hear that nothing is more fashionable than to keep people waiting. – None but vulgar persons pay any attention to punctuality. Is it not so, Millinette? [. . .] This mode of receiving visitors only upon one specified day of the week is a most convenient custom! It saves the trouble of keeping the house continually in order and of being always dressed. I flatter myself that I was the first to introduce it amongst the New York ee-light. You are quite sure that it is strictly a Parisian mode, Millinette? (*Aside.*) This girl is worth her weight in gold. – Millinette, how do you say armchair in French? [. . .] Fo-tool! That has a foreign – an out-of-the-wayish sound that is perfectly charming – and so genteel! There is something about our American words decidedly vulgar. Fowtool! How refined. Fowtool! Arm-chair! What a difference! [. . .] A woman of refinement and of fashion can always accommodate herself to everything foreign! And a week's study of that invaluable work, *French without a Master*, has made me quite at home in the court language of Europe! [. . .] What did you say was the name of this new servant, Millinette? [. . .] Ezekial, I suppose. Zeke! Dear me, such a vulgar name will compromise the dignity of the whole family. Can you not suggest something more aristocratic, Millinette? Something French! [. . .] A-dolph! Charming! Ring the bell, Millinette! I will change his name immediately, besides giving him a few directions.

Enter Zeke.

Your name, I hear, is Ezekial. – I consider it too plebeian an appellation to be uttered in my presence. In future you are called A-dolph. Don't reply – never interrupt me when I am speaking. A-dolph, as my guests arrive, I desire that you will inquire the name of every person, and then pronounce it in a loud, clear tone. That is the fashion in Paris. 〞

GLOSSARY

jenny-says-quoi i.e. *je-ne-sais-quoi*, indefinable quality
ee-light i.e. *élite*
fo-tool i.e. *fauteuil*, armchair (French)

Ghosts

Henrik Ibsen (1881), trans. Stephen Mulrine

WHO ☞ *Mrs Helene Alving, the widow of Captain Alving, a former court chamberlain.*

WHERE ☞ *In the drawing room of her house.*

TO WHOM ☞ *Pastor Manders, the same pastor who joined them in marriage twenty-nine years ago.*

WHEN ☞ *Contemporary with authorship.*

WHAT HAS JUST HAPPENED ☞ *Oswald Alving has returned home to visit his mother who sent him away as a young boy to prevent him from becoming morally corrupted by his father, Captain Alving. In order to prepare for the tenth anniversary of the captain's death, Pastor Menders has called to visit Mrs Alving. He needs to get things off his chest. He disapproves of Mrs Alving for not having lived a more conventional life and criticises her in the manner of the raising of her son. He calls her a bad mother for leaving her marriage only a year into it, having to be coerced – by him – into going back to it, and then for sending her son away to be educated. This is her response.*

WHAT SHE WANTS/OBJECTIVES TO PLAY ☞

- *To destroy the memory of her 'honourable' husband so she can in some private way break through the hypocrisy of the commemoration of his death.*

- *To put the record straight in the eyes of this rather stuffy and formal man who has had the audacity to reprimand her.*

- *To say out loud what has never been said in order to remove it from her life. It is a personal therapy, spoken for herself as much as for the Pastor.*

- *To establish and have recognised her achievements and her strength in handling the situation throughout the years.*

• *This piece has been assembled from the scene between Mrs Alving and Pastor Manders. Readers are advised to read the scene in its entirety in order to gain a thorough overview of the speech.*

Mrs Alving

❝ Well, you've said your piece. And tomorrow you'll make a speech in public, in memory of my husband. I won't be speaking tomorrow. But I will speak to you now, the way you have spoken to me.

All I wanted to say is that when you pass judgement on my married life, you're basing it on nothing more than popular opinion at the time.

The truth is my husband died just as depraved as he had been all his life.

After nineteen years of marriage, every bit as dissolute – in his desires at any rate – as he had been before you married us.

I'd managed to put up with it, though I knew perfectly well what was going on outside the house. But when he brought the scandal within these four walls . . . Yes, here, in our own home. In there . . . it was in the dining room I first found out about it. I was busy doing something in there, and the door was open. I heard our maid coming up from the garden, with some water for the flowers.

A short while after, I heard my husband come in. He said something to her in a low voice. Then I heard . . . (*A short laugh.*) Oh, it rings in my ears even now, heartbreaking, but at the same time so ridiculous . . . I heard my own servant say, 'Let me go, Mr Alving, please! Leave me alone!'

I knew soon enough what to believe. My husband had his way with the girl – and that affair had its consequences, Pastor Manders.

I've suffered a great deal in this house. To keep him at home in the evenings, and at nights, I had to join him in secret drinking bouts up in his room. I had to sit there with him, just the two of us, drinking, listening to his obscene, mindless talk, then end up wrestling with him, dragging him into his bed.

I had to, for my little boy's sake. Then came the crowning insult, when my own servant-girl . . . I swore then it would have to end! So now I seized power in my own house – absolute power. Power over him, and everything else besides. I had a weapon to use against him, you see, and he didn't dare say a word. That was when Oswald was sent away. He was going on for seven then, beginning to notice things and ask questions, the way children do. I couldn't bear that, Pastor Manders. I felt as if the child would be poisoned, just breathing the air of this polluted house. That's why I sent him away. You can understand too, why he was never allowed to set foot in this house, while his father was still alive. And what that cost me, no one knows.

I'd never have borne it if I hadn't had my work. Yes, I can safely say I've worked hard – all these additions to the property, all the improvements, all the innovations, for which Alving got the credit, of course – do you honestly think he had the initiative for these things? A man who used to lounge around on the sofa the whole day, reading an old court gazette? No, and I'll tell you something else – it was I who drove him on, during his more lucid intervals. And I had to bear the whole burden when he took to his debauched ways again or lapsed into abject self-pity. **99**

Miss Julie

August Strindberg (1888), *trans. Kenneth McLeish*

WHO ☞   *Miss Julie, or Lady Julie, 25 years old, the only daughter of his Lordship.*

WHERE ☞   *In the kitchen of a country estate in Sweden.*

TO WHOM ☞   *Jean, the personal manservant of her father, his Lordship.*

WHEN ☞   *On Midsummer Night, 1888.*

WHAT HAS JUST HAPPENED ☞   *Miss Julie has been alone in the kitchen with Jean for most of Midsummer Night, interrupted only occasionally by the cook. They have known each other since they were children though they have never, until this night, crossed the line into 'familiarity'. Having recently broken off an engagement, and always something of a wild woman, Julie has been throwing herself at Jean, trying to dominate him sexually – she is very much his social superior. Now that union has been consummated: accompanied by the sound of the local peasants with dancing and slanderous songs, Julie knows she has made herself forever vulnerable to everyone knowing of her sexual, and therefore social, transgression, and she is bitterly ashamed. She wants to run away with Jean, even though he has shown his true colours with a torrent of abuse, accusing her of letting down her class and of being a whore. She has started drinking, but wants to tell him her life story before, as she thinks, they will leave together.*

WHAT SHE WANTS/OBJECTIVES TO PLAY ☞

- *To explain herself by describing her upbringing, and by painting a picture of the world she was born into which gave her such confused ideas of gender equality.*
- *To win back the respect she believed he had for her.*
- *To warn him of what he has in store in a life with her.*
- *To let him know that she is not afraid and that she is more than a match for him.*

Miss Julie

" For a start, my mother wasn't a lady: just ordinary. She was brought up the way people were in those days: equality, freedom for women, all that. She hated the thought of marriage. When Papa proposed, she turned him down, but said he could be her lover. He promised her that he'd never allow his own wife to be treated any less respectfully than he was himself. She said she cared nothing for the world's opinion; he loved her; he accepted it. Soon he was barred from all his old friendships, trapped in domesticity, no satisfaction. I came into the world – an accident, I'm sure of that. Mama decided to bring me up like a child of nature, to make me learn everything a boy learned, to prove to the whole world that a woman was as good as a man. She dressed me in boy's clothes, forbade me the dairy, taught me riding and grooming and hunting. I even cut up the kill: disgusting. Ours was the estate where the men did women's work and the women did men's work – till naturally everything went to rack and ruin and everyone laughed at us. Finally Papa seemed to wake up – as if he'd been under a spell – and began asserting himself, insisting things were done his way. They never spoke after that. Mama fell ill – I don't know what it was. Fits. She hid in the attic or in the garden, she was often out all night. Then there was the fire – you must have heard abut it. Houses, stables, barns, all gone – and it can't have been accidental, as it happened the day after the insurance ran out, and the new premium was delayed in the post, so it arrived late.

She fills the glass and drinks.

[JEAN. You've had enough.
MISS JULIE. What if I have?]

We'd nothing. We had to sleep in the coaches. Papa didn't know where he could get cash to rebuild. He'd lost all his old friends; they'd forgotten him. Then Mama said he ought to try to borrow it from one of his old friends, a brick merchant from round here somewhere. Papa got the loan, and without interest. He was amazed. So the house was rebuilt.

She drinks again.

Guess who burned it down.

[JEAN: Your mother.]

Guess who the brick merchant was.

[JEAN: Her lover.]

Guess who the money belonged to.

[JEAN: Wha –? No idea.]

Mama.

[JEAN: Your father, surely, when he married her.
MISS JULIE. No,]

She kept their property separate. She'd money of her own, she didn't want Papa managing it, so she invested it with – her friend.

[JEAN. Who stole it.
MISS JULIE. Exactly.]

He held on to it. Papa found out. He couldn't take it to court, couldn't pay the lover, couldn't prove it was his wife's money. That's what she did to him. For making himself master of his own house. He tried to shoot himself, so they say. Missed. Well, in the end he came out of it, and made sure that Mama suffered for what she'd done. My first five years! I loved Papa, but I didn't know the whole story, so I sided with Mama. She taught me to hate all men – she wasn't fond of men – and I promised her never, never, to be a slave to any man. **99**

The Stronger

August Strindberg (1889), *trans. Michael Meyer*

WHO ☞   *Madame X, a young married actress, 20s plus.*

WHERE ☞   *The corner of a café, the kind 'frequented by
ladies'.*

TO WHOM ☞   *Mademoiselle Y, an unmarried actress. Though
the play is a two-hander, Madame Y never once speaks.*

WHEN ☞   *Contemporary with authorship.*

WHAT HAS JUST HAPPENED ☞   *Madame X, 'a married
actress', as Strindberg describes her in the cast list, enters a café
for hot chocolate on Christmas Eve; she is very properly attired
and carries gifts for her husband and children. She sees
Madamoiselle Y, sitting with a half-empty beer bottle in front
of her, leafing through magazines. She joins her at her table as it
is evident they know each other. Madame X has to this point
been trying to engage Madamoiselle Y in conversation – getting
nowhere, other than the occasional look and roar of laughter. She
has even invited her to join her and her family for dinner later
that evening. She suspects the silence is due to some professional
rivalry, but works out the truth during this speech.*

WHAT SHE WANTS/OBJECTIVES TO PLAY ☞

- *Initially to connect with this woman, to befriend her, to get an
  acknowledgement from her and to try to find out why things
  have always been tricky between them.*

- *After the realisation she wants to re-assert her control, to let
  her know that she, Madame X, is the stronger.*

- *To diminish her and to assault her with each moment's
  realisation.*

- *To let her know that she has known all along – on an
  emotional and fundamental level.*

Madame X

66 It's so strange about our friendship – when I first met
you, I was afraid of you, so afraid I didn't dare let you out of
my sight. Wherever I went, I took care to be near you – I
didn't dare become your enemy, so I became your friend. But
I always felt awkward when you came home to us, because I
saw my husband couldn't stand you – and then I felt
uncomfortable, as though my clothes didn't fit. I did everything to make him be nice to you, but without success. And
then you went off and got engaged. Then you and he became
great friends – as though you'd been afraid to show your true
feelings while you were uncommitted – and then – what
happened next? I didn't become jealous – funnily enough!
And I remember, when our first baby was christened, and
you stood as godmother, I made him kiss you – and he did,
but you got so upset – that is, I didn't notice it at the time –
I haven't thought of it since – haven't thought of it till –
now! (*Rises suddenly.*) Why are you so silent? You haven't said
a word all the time – you've just let me sit here talking!
You've sat there staring at me, winding all these thoughts out
of me like silk from a cocoon – thoughts – suspicions? Let
me see! Why did you break off your engagement? Why did
you never come and visit us after that? Why won't you come
and see us tonight?

Madamoiselle Y seems about to speak.

No! You don't need to say anything – I see it all now! So that
was why you – and why you – and why you -! Yes, of course!
Now it all adds up! So that was it! Ugh, I don't want to sit at
the same table as you!

Moves her things to the other table.

That was why I had to embroider tulips, which I hate, on his
slippers – because you liked tulips! That was why – (*Throws
slippers on the floor.*) – we had to spend our holiday at
Mälaren that summer, because you couldn't stand the sea –
that was why my son had to be called Eskil, because that was

your father's name – that was why I had to wear your colours, read your authors, eat your dishes, drink your drinks – your chocolate, for instance – that was why – oh, my God! – It's horrible, now I think of it – horrible! Everything, everything that belonged to you, entered into me. Even your passions! Your soul crept into mine like a worm into an apple, eating and eating, boring and boring, till there was nothing left but the skin and a little black mould. I wanted to run away from you, but I couldn't – you lay there like a snake with your black eyes, bewitching me – when I tried to use my wings they dragged me down. I lay in the water with my feet bound, and the more I tried to swim with my hands the deeper I sank, down, down, till I reached the bottom, where you lay like a giant crab ready to seize me in your claws! And I'm lying there now! **99**

Alan's Wife

Florence Bell and Elizabeth Robins (1893)

WHO ☞   *Jean, a young widow, 20s.*

WHERE ☞   *A room in Jean's cottage in the North of England.*

TO WHOM ☞   *Herself, her baby, and to God.*

WHEN ☞   *Contemporary with authorship.*

WHAT HAS JUST HAPPENED ☞   *Jean was married happily to Alan Creyke, a good but poor factory worker. He was killed in a factory accident whilst Jean was pregnant with their child. Time has passed: she has given birth to a physically disabled but seemingly sturdy child. She is severely depressed and has little to do with the care of the child. She loves him, but despairs of the life he will lead. She is alone, calling upon God to punish her, not the child. She feels her son is being punished for her constant happiness before Alan's death. During the speech she determines to smother her baby to death, which she does.*

WHAT SHE WANTS/OBJECTIVES TO PLAY ☞

- *To plea-bargain with God.*

- *To maintain her sanity.*

- *To find a way out of the horror that is the future for her.*

- *To protect her baby for the duration of his life.*

- *To justify the plan, forming in her mind, to suffocate her baby.*

Jean

“ Oh God! If I've been wicked, don't make it worse for the child – punish me some other way – don't hurt him any more – he's so little, dear God, – so helpless, and he never did any wrong! He hasn't been drunk with life and strength and love – he hasn't walked through the world exulting and fearless and forgetting You. That was I, oh, Father in heaven! Punish me and take the baby away. This is a hard place – this world down here. Take him away! (*She staggers to her feet – listens.*) He is stirring. (*Goes and looks in cradle – leans over it.*) Ah, how little you must know to be smiling in your sleep! (*Drops on her knees by the cradle.*) Dear little face! Ah! It's brave of you to smile when God has laid such heavy burdens on you! Do you think you will be able to smile later on when you see other boys running and leaping and being glad – when you're a man, dear, and see how good it is to be strong and fair? Can you bear it, little one? (*She rocks the cradle as if to hush him, though the child sleeps on – she croons drearily.*) Never mind, never mind! Mother'll be always at your side – always – always. Always? (*She stops, horror-stricken.*) Who can say so? I might die! It's natural I should go first and leave him to the mercy of – Oh, I cannot! I dare not! (*Bows her head over the cradle's edge – then half recovering, and yet with suppressed wildness whispers.*) Baby, I'm frightened! Listen, I don't know what to do. Do you want to live? Tell me, shall you ever hate me for this horrible gift of life? (*With wide vacant eyes.*) Oh, I seem to see you in some far-off time, your face distorted like your body, but with bitterness and loathing, saying, 'Mother, how could you be so cruel as to let me live and suffer? You could have eased my pain; you could have saved me this long martyrdom; when I was little and lay in your arms. Why didn't you save me? You were a coward – a coward.' (*She bows her head over the cradle again, overcome, then she lifts a drawn white face.*) It would be quite easy – only to cover the dear little face for a little while – only to shut out the air and light for a little while, and remember I'm fighting for his release. Yes, it would be quite easy – if only one's heart didn't sink and one's brain grow numb! (*Leans against the cradle, faint – her eyes fall on the child.*) Are your lips moving, dear? (*Pause.*) Are you asking for life? No, you don't want to live do you? No, no, you cannot! Darling, it will be so easy – you'll never know – it will only be that you'll go on sleeping – sleeping, until you wake up in heaven! **99**

An Ideal Husband

Oscar Wilde (1895)

WHO ☞   *Mrs Cheveley, a lady of society, 30s plus.*

WHERE ☞   *The Octagon drawing room at Sir Robert Chiltern's house, in a smart part of London.*

TO WHOM ☞   *Sir Robert.*

WHEN ☞   *Contemporary with authorship.*

WHAT HAS JUST HAPPENED ☞   *Sir Robert Chiltern, an important member of the House of Commons, and his wife, Lady Gertrude Chiltern, are hosting a gathering of the genteel London high society. During the evening, Mrs Cheveley, a long-time enemy of Lady Chiltern's, finds Sir Robert alone and attempts to blackmail him into supporting (and more importantly, convincing Parliament to support) a fraudulent scheme to build a canal in Argentina. Many years ago Mrs Cheveley's late mentor, Baron Arnheim, paid Sir Robert a healthy sum to sell him a Cabinet secret that suggested he buy stocks in the Suez Canal three days before the British government bought it; Mrs Cheveley has a letter as proof of his wrong doings. Here she reminds him, most eloquently, that he has no option other than to fulfil her wishes.*

WHAT SHE WANTS/OBJECTIVES TO PLAY ☞

- *To give him no choice but to comply with her needs by playing this political game with her.*

- *To be treated as a superior by him.*

- *To condemn the hypocrisy of English society.*

- *To not be judged – in making money out of this deal, she is behaving no worse than he did years ago: they are both opportunists in her eyes.*

- *To disempower him and remind him, in no uncertain terms, what a vulnerable position he is in.*

Mrs Cheveley

66 You know you are standing on the edge of a precipice. And it is not for you to make terms. It is for you to accept them. Supposing you refuse –

[SIR ROBERT CHILTERN. What then?]

My dear Sir Robert, what then? You are ruined, that is all! Remember to what point your Puritanism in England has brought you. In old days nobody pretended to be a bit better than his neighbours. In fact, to be a bit better than one's neighbours was considered excessively vulgar and middle-class. Nowadays, with our modern mania for morality, every-one has to pose as a paragon of purity, incorruptibility, and all the other seven deadly virtues – and what is the result? You all go over like ninepins – one after the other. Not a year passes in England without somebody disappearing. Scandals used to lend charm, or at least interest, to a man – now they crush him. And yours is a very nasty scandal. You couldn't survive it. If it were known that as a young man, secretary to a great and important minister, you sold a Cabinet secret for a large sum of money, and that was the origin of your wealth and career, you would be hounded out of public life, you would disappear completely. And after all, Sir Robert, why should you sacrifice your entire future rather than deal diplomatically with your enemy? For the moment, I am your enemy. I admit it! And I am much stronger than you are. The big battalions are on my side. You have a splendid position, but it is your splendid position that makes you so vulnerable. You can't defend it! And I am in attack. Of course I have not talked morality to you. You must admit in fairness that I have spared you that. Years ago you did a clever, unscrupulous thing; it turned out a great success. You owe it to your fortune and position. And now you have got to pay for it. Sooner or later we have all to pay for what we do. You have to pay now. Before I leave you tonight, you have got to promise me to suppress your report, and to speak in the House in favour of this scheme. [. . .] Those are my terms. 99

Uncle Vanya

Anton Chekhov (1897), *trans. Stephen Mulrine*

WHO ☞   *Yelena, 27.*

WHERE ☞   *The drawing room of her home, which is a remote farm in the Ukraine.*

TO WHOM ☞   *To herself.*

WHEN ☞   *Contemporary with authorship.*

WHAT HAS JUST HAPPENED ☞   *Yelena is married to Serebryakov, who has a daughter, Sonya, by his first marriage. Yelena is more like an elder sister to her. They live in a stultified world of meaningless inertia. Barely a life at all, the men drinking, the women 'drifting about, doing nothing'. Though bored by her husband's endless demands and neediness, she is not able to return Sonya's Uncle Vanya's declaration of love for her. But when Sonya confesses her all-consuming love for Astrov, the visiting physician, Yelena realises she may be a little in love with Astrov herself. Yelena has just promised to sound Astrov out, though she already knows he is not interested in Sonya. She is alone when she speaks.*

WHAT SHE WANTS/OBJECTIVES TO PLAY ☞

- *To make sense of the grim world in which they live.*

- *To support Sonya – and not become a sexual rival for Astrov's love. And she knows she would win any such contest hands down, crushing Sonya.*

- *To justify her own marriage to herself, in relationship to the tedious context of her life.*

- *To say out loud what she could not say just now to Sonya.*

- *To find the courage to be set free from this dreary existence.*

- *To entertain, fleetingly, the possibility that her feelings might be reciprocated.*

Yelena

" There's nothing worse than knowing somebody else's secret, and not being able to help. (*Musing.*) He's not in love with her, that's obvious, but why shouldn't he marry her? She's not attractive, but for a country doctor, someone of his age, she'd make an excellent wife. Intelligent, extremely kind, innocent . . . No, that's not the point . . . (*A pause.*) I understand that poor girl. In the midst of this desperate boredom, surrounded by grey shadows wandering in and out, instead of human beings, listening to vulgar chit-chat from people who know nothing but eating, drinking and sleeping – now and again he appears, so different from the rest, handsome, interesting, attractive, like a bright moon rising in the darkness . . . To fall under the spell of such a man, to forget oneself . . . I think I'm a little in love myself. Yes, I'm bored when he's not here, and just look at me, smiling when I think of him. Uncle Vanya says I have mermaid's blood in my veins. 'Let yourself go even just once in your life' . . . Well? Perhaps that's what I should do . . . just fly away, free as a bird, away from all of you, away from your sleepy faces, and your talk, just forget you even exist . . . But I'm too cowardly, too timid . . . My conscience would torment me . . . Yet he comes here every day, I can guess why, and I already feel guilty . . . I feel like kneeling before Sonya and begging her forgiveness, crying . . . **"**

The Dance of Death, Part Two

August Strindberg (1901), *trans. Stephen Mulrine*

WHO ☞ *Alice, early 40s, though could be played younger. Wife to the tyrannous Captain and cousin to Kurt the Quarantine Master in whose home this scene is set.*

WHERE ☞ *The exquisitely decorated and furnished drawing room.*

TO WHOM ☞ *Allan, Kurt's son. They are alone.*

WHEN ☞ *Contemporary with authorship.*

WHAT HAS JUST HAPPENED ☞ *Alice's only daughter, Judith, has been flirting with Allan mercilessly, whom she knows to be in love with her. She has been playing games, even flirting with the visiting Lieutenant in front of him, whom she is also driving mad with desire. Allan has just rushed into the room, crying into one of Judith's perfumed handkerchiefs. He doesn't know where he stands with Judith and is having his heart broken by her, bit by agonising bit, but cannot resist. Alice knows her daughter's cruel ways: she has little love for her and knows how mercenary she is; Alice is more likely to align her affections where the money lies – the Colonel she refers to at the end of the speech is 60! Alice has been married for 25 years to a man who has made her life hell, a combative life of contemptuous loathing, bullying and persistent controlling; he is described as a vampire. But these feelings are mutual; the two of them are committed to dancing a sort of 'dance of death', to the bitter end. This has formed her attitude to men, even the young and innocent, which goes some way to explain the duality of her very contradictory temperament – and with that, her conflicting objectives.*

WHAT SHE WANTS/OBJECTIVES TO PLAY ☞

- *To give him a life lesson – albeit in a somewhat brutal and sadistic way.*

- *To warn him off her daughter, by letting him know what a heartless wretch she is.*

- *To make him believe she is a friend to him in the guise of consolation.*

- *To let him know and trust that she, above all others, understands the pains of unreciprocated love. So lulling him into a sense of safety around her.*

- *To hurt him, she later blurts out her love for him, though there has been no overt sign of it to this point, so maybe she is punishing him here for not feeling all this for her, the mother of the love object!*

- *To make a man of him, she despises weak men, or at least men who cannot see what is actually going on. And then to make a child of him when she patronisingly dismisses him at the end.*

- *To destabilise him.*

Alice

Alice thinks for a few moments, then begins writing. Allan suddenly rushes in without seeing Alice, flings himself down on the sofa, and sobs uncontrollably into a lace handkerchief. Alice observes him for a while, then gets up and goes over to the sofa.

66 (*Gently.*) Allan . . .

Allan sits up, embarrassed, and tries to hide the handkerchief behind his back.

(*Gentle, feminine, with genuine concern.*) You mustn't be afraid of me, Allan – you're in no danger from me. What's the matter? Aren't you feeling well?

[ALLAN. No.]

What is it?

[ALLAN. I don't know.]

Have you a headache?

[ALLAN. No, I haven't.]

Is it your heart? Are you in pain?

[ALLAN. Yes.]

Pain, terrible pain – as if your heart were melting away! And something tugging at it, tearing it apart . . .

[ALLAN. How do you know?]

And you want to die, you wish you were dead, everything seems so impossible. And all you can think of is one thing – one person. But if two people can only think of the same person, then one of them is headed for sorrow.

Allan is picking abstractedly at his handkerchief.

It's a sickness, and there's no cure for it. You can't eat, you don't want to drink, all you want to do is weep – so bitterly. You'd like to hide away in the forest, where nobody can see you, because it's the kind of affliction people laugh at – people are so cruel! Ugh! And what is it you want from her? Nothing! You don't want to kiss her lips, because you know you'd die if you did. Whenever your thoughts fly to her, you can feel death drawing nearer. And it truly is death, my child – the death that brings life. But you don't understand that yet. There's a scent of violets – it's her!

Goes up to Allan and gently takes the handkerchief from him.

Yes, it's her – she's everywhere, she and she alone! Oh, you poor boy!

Allan can do nothing but bury his face in her lap.

You poor, poor boy! Oh, how painful it all is!

She dries his tears with the handkerchief.

There, there! Yes, cry – cry all you want. You'll feel better for it – it'll ease the pain in your heart. But now you must stand up, Allan, and be a man – Otherwise she won't give you a second glance! That cruel girl, who isn't really cruel! Has she been tormenting you? With the Lieutenant? Then listen to me, my boy – You've got to make friends with the Lieutenant, so you can talk about her together – that'll help a little too.

[ALLAN. I don't even want to look at the Lieutenant!]

Listen, silly – it won't be long before the Lieutenant comes to see you, to discuss her with you! Because . . . (*Allan looks up, hopefully.*) Shall I be kind and tell you why? (*Allan nods.*) Because he's just as miserable as you!

[ALLAN (*brightening*). Really?]

He certainly is, and whenever Judith hurts his feelings, he needs someone to bare his soul to. There – you're looking more cheerful already!

[ALLAN. Doesn't she want the Lieutenant?]

She doesn't want either of you, my dear – she wants the Colonel! (*Allan looks thoroughly miserable.*) What, the water works again? Well, you're not getting this handkerchief back – Judith likes to hang onto her belongings, and she has a round dozen of these! (*Allan is crestfallen.*) I'm afraid that's just the way she is. Now, sit over there while I write another letter, then you can run an errand for me. **))**

Fanny's First Play

George Bernard Shaw (1911)

WHO ☞   *Margaret, 18.*

WHERE ☞   *In the drawing room.*

TO WHOM ☞   *Her mother.*

WHEN ☞   *Contemporary with authorship.*

WHAT HAS JUST HAPPENED ☞   *In this play within a play, written by the Fanny of the title, Margaret is responding to her mother, who has accused her of being 'hardened' – meaning in this time, cold, modern and immune to the sensibilities of her class – which is upper-middle. Two weeks ago, Margaret found herself at a dance when a police raid took place. Innocent men and women were herded out onto the street and attacked – based on nothing more than assumptions that the women were morally loose and the gentlemen likely to be no better. In self-defence, Margaret punched an officer, knocking out two teeth. She is taken to gaol, where she sleeps soundly with others – suffragettes and more hardened criminals – and has no shame about what she did, nor about the penalties she suffered. Having witnessed such injustice and challenged it, she now feels alive and real – for the first time in her life. She is liberated from the hypocrisy of her class and is at peace. She has now returned home to her parents who are shocked, both with the news of what has happened, and with their daughter's new take on life.*

WHAT SHE WANTS/OBJECTIVES TO PLAY ☞

- *To let her mother know that she, Margaret, is changed for ever, and she is truly free.*

- *To separate from her family and all it represents to her.*

- *To speak to her mother as a fellow adult, for the first time, with a new sense of who she is, but with no sense of who her mother is: she is almost a stranger.*

- *To experience once again the sheer exhilaration of speaking her mind – of saying the unexpected, of going against the grain.*

- *To scorn her mother, rejecting any further parental control, and making it clear that any efforts to mould her into the 'ideal' daughter have failed.*

Margaret

❝ I'm not hardened, mother. But I can't talk nonsense about it. You see, it's all real to me. I've suffered it. I've been shoved and bullied. I've had my arms twisted. I've been made to scream with pain in other ways. I've been flung into a filthy cell with a lot of other poor wretches as if I were a sack of coals being emptied into a cellar. And the only difference between me and the others was that I hit back. Yes I did. And I did worse. I wasn't ladylike. I cursed. I called names. I heard words that I didn't even know that I knew, coming out of my mouth just as if somebody else had spoken them. The policeman repeated them in court. The magistrate said he could hardly believe it. The policeman held out his hand with his two teeth in it that I knocked out. I said it was all right; that I had heard myself using those words quite distinctly; and that I had taken the good conduct prize for three years running at school. The poor old gentleman put me back for the missionary to find out who I was, and to ascertain the state of my mind. I wouldn't tell, of course, for your sakes at home here; and I wouldn't say I was sorry, or apologise to the policeman, or compensate him or anything of that sort. I wasn't sorry. The one thing that gave me any satisfaction was getting in that smack on his mouth; and I said so. So the missionary reported that I seemed hardened and that no doubt I would tell who I was after a day in prison. Then I was sentenced. So now you see I'm not a bit the sort of girl I thought myself. And I don't know what sort of person you really are, or what sort of person father really is. [. . .]

You shouldn't have prayed for me to be enlightened if you didn't want me to be enlightened. If the truth were known,

I suspect we all want our prayers to be answered only by
halves: the agreeable halves. Your prayer didn't get answered
by halves, mother. You've got more than you bargained for
in the way of enlightenment. I shall never be the same again.
I shall never speak in the old way again. I've been set free
from this silly little hole of a house and all its pretences.
I know now that I am stronger than you and Papa. I haven't
found that happiness of yours that is within yourself; but
I've found strength. For good or evil I am set free; and none
of the things that used to hold me can hold me now. **99**

The Apple Cart

George Bernard Shaw (1929)

WHO ☞   *Orinthia, young mistress to King Magnus,*
20s plus.

WHERE ☞   *In Orinthia's domestic quarters.*

TO WHOM ☞   *King Magnus, her lover.*

WHEN ☞   *England of 1962*

WHAT HAS JUST HAPPENED ☞   *Set in an imaginary future,*
King Magnus is a popular King of England who finds himself in
conflict with the Prime Minister and his corrupt Cabinet who are
determined to deprive him of the right to influence public opinion
and instead wish to create a constitutional monarchy where he
has no rights at all, not even a royal veto. This is the political
context within which this domestic interlude of a scene takes
place. Although married to Queen Jemima, Magnus also has a
mistress, Orinthia, a woman with a fiery and engaging
temperament. They have been talking about how weak her two
previous husbands were: she is a divine thing whilst they were
merely mortal. Magnus taunts her with the idea that it must be
magnificent to have the consciousness of a goddess without ever
doing a thing to justify it. This is her response.

WHAT SHE WANTS/OBJECTIVES TO PLAY ☞

- *To use her considerable powers as a seductress to remind him*
  of her particular qualities; and to help illustrate her
  philosophy.

- *To tantalise him intellectually and tease him sensually.*

- *To show him a completely different way of viewing the world*
  and his subjects, and to make him question whether one can
  ever make a difference through one's actions.

- *To illustrate absolute contempt for those she considers beneath*
  her.

Orinthia

" Give me a Goddess's work to do; and I will do it. I will
even stoop to a queen's work if you will share the throne
with me. But do not pretend that people will become great
by doing great things. They do great things because they are
great, if the great things come along. But they are great just
the same when the great things do not come along. If I never
did anything but sit in this room and powder my face and tell
you what a clever fool you are, I should still be heavens high
above the millions of common women who do their domestic
duty, and sacrifice themselves, and run Trade departments
and all the rest of the vulgarities. Has all the tedious public
work you have done made you any the better? I have seen
you before and after your boasted strokes of policy; and you
were the same man, and would have been the same man to
me and to yourself if you had never done them. Thank God
my self-consciousness is something nobler than vulgar
conceit in having done something. It is what I am, not what
I do, that you must worship in me. If you want deeds, go to
your men and women of action, as you call them, who are all
in a conspiracy to pretend that the mechanical things they
do, the foolhardy way they risk their worthless lives, or their
getting up in the morning at four and working sixteen hours
a day for thirty years, like coral insects, make them great.
What are they for? These dull slaves? To keep the streets
swept for me. To enable me to reign over them in beauty like
the stars without having anything to do with their slavery
except to console it, to dazzle it, to enable them to forget it in
adoring dreams of me. Am I not worth it? Look into my eyes
and tell the truth. Am I worth it or not? **"**

Blood Wedding

Federico Garcia Lorca (1933), *trans. Tanya Ronder*

WHO ☞   *Bride, 20s.*

WHERE ☞   *In a 'white room', in the new marital home of the bride, in Andalucia, rural Spain.*

TO WHOM ☞   *Some women of the neighbourhood and the groom's mother.*

WHEN ☞   *Contemporary with authorship, though there is a surreal non-specific time quality about the setting.*

WHAT HAS JUST HAPPENED ☞   *Leonardo Feliza, now married, and the Bride, were once in love, but never married. He chooses this day, her marriage day to another, to take her away: she goes willingly. They know they cannot resist their fate. The Groom's mother is incandescent with rage, humiliation and shame, and the scorned Groom has run off to find Leonardo to even the score, which will surely result in his death. It is the following morning: her daughter-in-law arrives, unexpectedly alone. She needs to declare her purity and her innocence before meeting what she is sure will be her death too.*

The chorus of neighbours are trying to separate the warring women, as the Groom's mother lunges at her as soon as she sees her.

WHAT SHE WANTS/OBJECTIVES TO PLAY ☞

- *To set the record straight, to explain her motives, it is her testimony.*

- *To die with her purity, her reputation intact.*

- *To let the Groom's mother know how she recognised and valued the security offered by her son – and yet explain how he left her cold, both emotionally and physically.*

- *To be heard – and to try and express the physical longing, the sexual desire, that almost overwhelmed her, but which she managed to resist.*

- *To match her own courage against the alleged immeasurable courage of the Groom's mother.*

Bride

❝ Leave her! I've come so she can kill me and they can take me with the others. My flesh is still warm and it shouldn't be. (*To Mother.*) Not your hands though – go get some wire or a sickle. It has to be hard so the inside of me snaps (*To neighbour.*) Get off her! (*To Mother.*) It's meaningless, but I want you to know that I'm virgin. You can put me in the soil knowing that.

[MOTHER. Why are you telling me? Why is she telling me this?]

Because I left with another man. That's what I did. Maybe you would have too.

[MOTHER. Take her away.]

I was sick! I'd been too close to the fire. I was sick from that time. I thought your boy, your son, my husband I chose for myself, would help. Cool me. Be my balm. He was perfect. A glass of clean, clear water. Who might bring children, land, health and I wanted him.

[MOTHER. But –]

Leonardo screamed out to me and now I think he always would. He set a thousand birds off to stop me on my way. He bubbled like a river across the plain. Full of weeds and tress and dark tuneless songs. I didn't want him! I didn't choose him! I wanted yours. I wanted your son. He was my future, my end, believe me! I was dragged by Leonardo, a wave, a nature I couldn't hold off. I would always have heard his moan in that dark filthy river. I think I hated him. I couldn't keep away! If all the babies of your son's sons were hanging off my balding hair, I would go to him, that's the truth. I'd always have left. **❞**